# CONSENTING TO GOD
# AS GOD IS

# CONSENTING TO GOD AS GOD IS

*Thomas Keating*

LANTERN BOOKS ✦ NEW YORK

*A Division of Booklight Inc.*

2016

Lantern Books

128 Second Place

Brooklyn, NY 11231

www.lanternbooks.com

All biblical quotations are from the New Revised Standard
Version of the Bible copyright © 1989 by the Division of Christian
Education of the National Council of Churches of Christ in the
United States of America.

Cover photograph by W. T. Bryant

Library of Congress Cataloging-in-Publication Data

Names: Keating, Thomas.
Title: Consenting to God as God is / Thomas Keating.
Description: New York : Lantern Books, 2016. | Includes
bibliographical references.
Identifiers: LCCN 2015031350 | ISBN 9781590565292 (pbk. : alk.
paper) | ISBN 9781590565308 (ebook)
Subjects: LCSH: Contemplation. | Prayer—Christianity.
Classification: LCC BV5091.C7 K4134 2016 | DDC 248.3/4—dc23
LC record available at http://lccn.loc.gov/2015031350

**To the ECI Council members, past and present.**

*You are the cutting edge of the expansion of Contemplative Outreach into the Spanish and Portuguese speaking world, and a shining light for the dynamic unfolding of the entire Contemplative Outreach organism toward its transformative purpose and goal, which is to offer the human family a way to the precious experience of being loved by God.*

# ACKNOWLEDGMENTS

My deep thanks to Isabel Castellanos for the encouragement, support, and editorial services that brought this book into being. Thanks also to Gail Fitzpatrick-Hopler for help in editing, and to Martin Rowe and Gene Gollogly at Lantern Books for their work on preparing this book for production.

# CONTENTS

PART III

# INTRODUCTION

BETWEEN JANUARY 2007 and April 2009, I met in Miami for several days during each year with the members of the council for Extensión Contemplativa Internacional. ECI is the Spanish and Portuguese branch of Contemplative Outreach. Their mission is to contribute to the renewal of the contemplative dimension of the Gospel in the Spanish- and Portuguese-speaking world.

At these informal gatherings in which we lived and prayed together, I offered daily presentations on various aspects of the spiritual journey. *Consenting to God As God Is* is a collection of those intimate talks. Each year, we explored together a specific topic or theme. The three sections of this book correspond to each of those annual themes.

The material contained in this volume is addressed to people who have been practicing centering prayer for several years, who are familiar with its immediate conceptual background, and who are already serving in Contemplative Outreach and ECI. Hence the content may not be appropriate for those who are just beginning to practice centering prayer. Other books, such as *Open Mind, Open Heart* and *Intimacy with God*, may serve them better at this initial stage. This book is addressed primarily to people with some personal experience of the spiritual journey and especially to those engaged in some form of contemplative service.

A word about the title: *Consenting to God as God Is* is a way of describing the most fundamental exercise of Christian faith. This exercise recognizes the illusory character of our past ideas of God and gives birth to a new understanding that leads to a deep conversion of the heart. We realize that God wills to give himself to us, and that he is seeking the complete gift of ourselves in return. Along with centering prayer, we consent and surrender to God's presence and action within all our activities. ◆

**Thomas Keating**

—January 2016

# PART I

---

## CONSENTING
## TO
## CONTEMPLATIVE
## SERVICE

By 2007, the practice of centering prayer was growing in an increasing number of Latin American countries. Books and materials had already been translated into Spanish and Portuguese, and members of the ECI board had received training as presenters following the model used by Contemplative Outreach in our English-speaking communities. I sensed that a certain rigidity had seeped into their transmission and I invited them to meet with me in Miami for a few days to explore this issue. This gathering, and the two that followed it in successive years, took place in the private home of one of the ECI members. There we shared prayer, food, and the Eucharist, and also shared deeply about the need for flexibility and cultural understanding in our service.

We also examined the possibility of engaging the ECI Board in a contemplative form of governance. Shortly after this gathering, the ECI Board changed its name to ECI Council and began experimenting with a nonhierarchical governance structure that has matured over the years and continues to this day.

# 1

# REFLECTIONS ON THE GLOBAL MISSION AND SERVICE OF CONTEMPLATIVE OUTREACH

IN SPITE OF their avowed purpose of promoting peace and justice, the religions of the world have made major contributions to the violence in human history. Religions are constituted of people with false selves. We know what the false self is from our own personal experience. The great treasure that interreligious dialogue among the world religions could unlock is to enable people to get to know and love other religions and the people who practice them. The attitude of exclusivity that has characterized religions from their beginning must be laid to rest. God is too big to be contained in one religion. Contemplative Outreach is a voice crying in the wilderness of the violence and disunity that still exists among the religions of the world.

Contemplative prayer as the special gift from God is one that *has been given*. The proper response to this gift is to consent to God's presence and action manifested in us by the desire for God, or simply by the desire for happiness and the willingness to take practical steps to explore the behavior that leads to it.

The purpose of Contemplative Outreach is to guide people attracted to the Christian understanding of the practice of contemplative transformation. The centering prayer method, which is the center of this process, cultivates an attitude of total receptivity to God by consenting to God's presence and action within. Growing in interior silence seems to be the best means of opening to the divine presence as we move inwardly to "pray in secret," as Jesus invites us in Matthew 6:6.

What Contemplative Outreach is trying to transmit is something greater than any one religion. Human beings at their root are contemplative. Other religions are also serving the awakening of that transformative movement that goes with all humans born into this world. The contemplative life is the heart of the world. In becoming a contemplative, one manifests the face of God more vigorously than in the practice of one's religion without that dimension.

It is urgent and crucial that we make this basic teaching available in every language and in every culture. The method of centering prayer is in the service of awakening this innate capacity of human nature, which has the Holy Spirit as its source. If we can connect people to the Holy Spirit, we can offer people a means by which they can choose to be transformed by consenting to the action of the Holy Spirit within them.

The Catholic tradition has a rich teaching about the mystical life and its stages and difficulties. Contemporary psychology has reinforced the teaching about the dark side of humanity that some in psychological circles call the "shadow," and which in theological language form the three consequences of original sin. These are *illusion*—not knowing what happiness is; *concupiscence*—looking for it in the wrong places; and *weakness of will*—the experience that we cannot change or heal our unmanageable lives without the grace of God. The fact that we cannot fix anybody, not even ourselves, is itself a precious insight. There are negative energies deep within us that we are not even aware of. The shadow side is extremely subtle and can even get into ministry in various ways. It can also insinuate itself into one's prayer life; hence the urgent need of purification, or what John the Baptist called *repentance*.

The Christmas liturgy reveals the spiritual life through the language of symbol and liturgical rituals. As a manifestation of their sacred desire, the Magi, who hold a prominent place in the Christmas liturgy, came from the ends of the earth to Israel in search of the messiah. They represent genuine seekers of the truth from every time and place. After immense difficulties and trials they found the Babe of Bethlehem, the Source of all creation, in a manger.

The message that John the Baptist first articulated is one way to move from an exclusively self-centered life into the transformative destiny that God has prepared for us. The term "repentance" in scripture is primarily the *willingness to change the direction in which we are looking for happiness.* This calls upon us to surrender completely to the interior purification of our deep-seated selfishness, including of our desire to *feel God* in prayer.

There is concern that the teaching regarding centering prayer be done correctly. Actually, it is not so much the letter of the teaching as *the being of the teachers who transmit it* that is most important. They know it in such a way through experience that they can never quite explain it. If our concern that centering prayer be properly transmitted becomes an anxiety, we can be pretty sure that we have an issue with control. The desire to control and its frustration may be the secret cause of the anxiety.

The purpose of trials, disappointments, and worries, from God's perspective, is to free us from all anxiety. We never quite heal the false self and its attachment to the fundamental instinctual tendencies of human nature. As long as we live, God keeps lovingly, but relentlessly, bringing to our attention everything that is an obstacle to pure love.

Saint Thérèse of Lisieux did not pray for the love of God that she could feel, but that God might give her *his own love* with which to love him. Notice that her confidence was not based on any act of her own, but instead on her surrender to divine love. She received one of the greatest graces that accompanies the mystical life, which is called the "wound of love." Saint Teresa of Ávila experienced it as the piercing of her heart by an arrow. The Blessed Mother experienced it as a sword. Evidently, there are different degrees of this "wound of love."

To be overly concerned about our ministry is easy and the symptoms are obvious. You are obsessed by difficulties and the inner feeling of failure that you just can't shake. Whatever faults you can't easily release should have top priority in your letting-go process, because that is what enables the space inside to open to God's presence, which is the substance of contemplative life. It can take many forms, but the essence of it is a longing for God's presence that follows us around from morning to night, and which is only obscured when the residue of the false self manifests itself. Some of that residue lingers in the unconscious from early childhood, especially as a result of traumatic experiences like rejection, neglect, lack of acceptance and affection, and over-severity. For example, suppose you are an approval bug by temperament, and, because of its lack in early life, you are always seeking more affection and approval. To try to please everybody is characteristic of that particular energy center. To let go of that desire is a great leap into freedom.

The truth is that pleasing others is often a kind of obsession. Bill W., the cofounder of Alcoholics Anonymous, said that he suffered from depression for most of his adult life.

Only toward the end did he discover that the desire to please everyone and its inevitable frustration were the real sources of his depression. He had recovered from alcoholism, but not from its cause, which was his attachment to pleasing others.

The psychological consequence of how the false self works with the instinctual desires for affection and esteem, security and survival, and power and control is the awareness of what daily life is also continually pointing out to us. The attachment that we experience to one or all of these emotional programs for happiness, which set off negative emotions when they are frustrated, is gradually unloaded through the purification process. But God does not seem to be satisfied with that. He keeps moving to more intimate levels of attachment, because *de*tachment from our desires brings the ultimate freedom that will enable us to be transformed and our ministry to be most effective.

Of course, in daily life difficulties will continue to come up. When you finally hit bottom, God will start functioning in a substantial way. The full force of God's help is most available when all human help has been exhausted.

Contemplation in prayer and practice is in the service of this detachment. If detachment is not sufficient, the false self will get in the way of relationships, and these can be especially delicate when it comes to people of another culture or religion. Detachment from our inmost selves is the key to hearing what people of the local culture are saying or expecting, whether they are of a conservative or a liberal frame of mind.

The application of this teaching and the experience of centering prayer together with the seeming failure, weariness, or all the other difficulties that accompany ministry, are not only for the benefit of the people you are serving. They are for *your* benefit. God will turn the world upside down in order to bring one person to full transformation in Christ.

The human family as a whole is meant for transformation. That state of consciousness manifests the glory of God like nothing else can do. When we pray for God's glory, we are also praying for detachment from ourselves, so that God's presence may pour through us as a channel. A good practice is regularly to take stock of the things that are annoying us the most and to see if the cause might be something that we are not quite ready to let go of.

What do we mean and intend when we say that Contemplative Outreach is committed as a spiritual organism to maintaining the integrity of the centering prayer practice? I can think of three points. The first one is that the centering prayer method and its immediate conceptual background are contained in the vision of Contemplative Outreach and the refined essentials of the Contemplative Outreach introductory program. Second, practices for daily life such as the Welcoming Prayer Practice, *lectio divina*, and other workshops are not part of the integrity of the method, but offer skillful means to bring its effects into daily life. That means that you choose what practices might be helpful for you. Some of them are useful for some, but not for others. Finally, and this is perhaps the most important point: apart from my foundational work *Open Mind, Open Heart*, books, tapes, and articles offer further support for the conceptual background of centering prayer, but are not part of the integrity of the method and its immediate conceptual background. Rather, they invite the creativity of future contributors in order to integrate centering prayer into specific cultural, theological, and spiritual situations. Thus, flexibility and creativity are just as important as adherence to the basic principles, provided they come from people who have enough experience of the practice and whose manner of life reflects it.

We must not adhere too closely to the letter of the guidelines or teach the "refined essentials" in such a way as to leave no room for exceptions. We are offering a method that works for most people most of the time; that's what a *guideline* is as distinguished from a *rule*. A guideline is a prudent way of going about something rather than a law or a rule.

If we were raised in a culture ruled by kings or dictators, we have a hierarchical superego, so to speak, and a loyalty to the written word that may be compulsive. It is a beautiful thing to be loyal and grateful for something that we have benefited from. But it is not God. God does not feel bound by any means including the best means, and so in certain circumstances we have to listen to what the culture is saying. We must really *hear* the difficulties that meditators see in our teaching and have a positive and encouraging attitude toward the experience of the people we are teaching. We may have a reasonable concern that they are getting it right, or in the case of presenters, whether they are presenting it accurately. But this is where we have to give the Spirit the chance to show us that there are other ways of meditating than ours. And, of course, there are other excellent methods that are now available, like that of Dom John Main, practiced by the World Community for Christian Meditation.

Once in a while you may encounter persons who have been in another tradition or who have been exposed to prayer or meditation for a long time. In both cases they may have experienced similar forms of meditation oriented to contemplative prayer before coming to us. Their experience needs to be respected. The Spirit may be asking us to deal prudently with their situation and support it as much as we can, and if we make a mistake, we leave it to God to fix. Certain situations require an exception to what we usually ask people to do. The way that divine wisdom works in us is not always the path of conforming to a particular way of doing things.

The spirit of Extensión Contemplativa Internacional and the application of it to our mission requires a great sensitivity to these circumstances, offering what new people actually ask for without insisting on anything more. If they are benefiting from what we are offering, they will ask for more. And if they wander off on their own, that is their choice.

More and more frequently, Contemplative Outreach and Extensión Contemplativa Internacional are being called to share the ways in which the Spirit communicates through the centering prayer practice with a world and people in desperate need. We must find compassionate and culturally sensitive means of reaching out to them. ➤

2

# RESPONDING TO OUR PERSONAL VOCATION

WHILE WE ARE building a constituency that reaches out geographically, you might also think of what you want to do personally. Think of Paul's example of the Body of Christ and the cells in that Body. The human body is a kind of paradigm of the spiritual communion of the human family with God. A sense of vocation may arise as time goes on. You may experience a calling for what you can contribute to this building up of the Body of Christ.

If you can figure out what you want to do, like to do, and have the talent to do, then why not do it? Every cell in the human body has its purpose: it has a *vocation*, to put it in spiritual terms. Contemplative Outreach is an organ in the Body of Christ, which comprises all of humanity, past, present, and to come.

There are varieties of duties in Christ's body. Saint Paul points out that some are apostles, some are teachers, some have a charismatic gift, but all are being moved by the Spirit

and drawn to contribute to a special need in Christ's Body
(see 1 Corinthians 12:28). To follow that attraction is a more
effective way of exercising leadership than to set out with a
plan of one's own.

There are many ways of serving in the organism we call
Contemplative Outreach. One of the things we need most
is good facilitators. That is to say, people who can lead a
small group, have a sense of where the group is, and what
the situation might require next. A leader in the Body of
Christ is a servant. It does not matter so much *what* we do.
What matters is that we do what we feel an attraction to
do, which other people confirm by urging us to do it and by
supporting us in our work.

It is not easy to communicate this vision to the groups
that are beginning to form in different countries. In Latin
America, as in other parts of the western world, organizations
tend to have a hierarchical structure. Leadership for such
folk means a top–down set of prescriptions. In our case,
leadership does not consist of exercising authority in this
way. Instead, leadership in our case involves serving the
spread of the vision of Contemplative Outreach with the
particular gifts that God has given us. As Paul points out,
we can't say to our bodily members, "We don't need the
hand or we don't need the foot" (see 1 Corinthians 12:21).
The body needs all its parts, including the humbler ones.
There is no room in the developing communities for the
kind of ego that says, "I will fix everybody's problems."

This mind-set needs to be gently but firmly replaced with one that perceives that service of the vision is not something that we initiate. Rather, we feel ourselves being called with our particular talents, gifts, and background to offer a service that perhaps no one else can provide, at least not for now. And it is in finding out what that is and doing it that we are most likely to be effective as well as at peace in the services we offer.

Actually, the primary act of leadership that anybody can perform for us is doing centering prayer twice daily and letting ourselves be led into the mystery of God within us. Once in a while, we get a sense of what this may look like. For instance, when a group is gathered on a retreat, in a formation workshop, or during a presenter's training course, you may notice that someone may ask a question or make a little joke, and the whole group moves into a new spiritual place. There is no up or down in the spiritual life, but there can be a sense of moving to a new perspective. The group might be on the level of evaluating whether they like this or that in your teaching, when all of a sudden the whole atmosphere shifts without our doing anything. The Spirit casts a mysterious covering over the assembly and everybody moves into a new space at once.

The covering is a symbol of the spiritual space in which everybody is united beyond any rational kind of explanation. It unites people in an experience that is refreshing and delightful. This is a communication of the Spirit. It may be what Saint John the Evangelist, in one of his letters, calls the "anointing of the Spirit," and which teaches you everything you need to know. The anointing of the Spirit is a trans-rational experience that is both a knowledge of God without concepts and a sense of the intimate presence of God in faith. When it is very strong, it may be what Saint John calls the glory of God. The glory of God is the divine presence when it is *perceived* by us.

This is the best kind of teaching because it is not our teaching, nor is it anything we learned from a book. It is the fact that through our practice and the preparation of our rational faculties, we let go of our preoccupations and their tendencies to dominate our attention, and with the support of others in the group receive a brief but strong sense of what the Kingdom of God really is. It is not something we can fake, but something we may slip into when we are not doing something else.

It may also happen in private prayer. As you are sitting there, letting thoughts go by, some of them will be pounding you in one way or another or exerting their obsessive and compulsive qualities. And then for some reason unbeknownst to us, the Spirit gives us a little nudge, and all of a sudden we are in a different and wonderful place interiorly. We may be confused, doubting, completely distracted, or bored to death, when in a flash, we are in a new and wonderful awareness. This shift of presence is the movement of the Spirit within us. This kind of attentiveness is not the same as attention, which is to a particular experience. Attentiveness is a broad and unlimited kind of perception or experience: a spaciousness, you might say, in which everything is contained. You do not think of any particular "thing." It is a movement from "things" to what *is*.

What is the amount of time to give to centering prayer? It depends on your other duties. If you are retired, you have more freedom, and it would be good to add a little more time for prayer, like increasing it to an hour twice a day. If you are engaging in *lectio divina* regularly, you might think of establishing a daily practice of forty minutes of centering prayer and then another twenty minutes of *lectio*. It is hard for some people to find this amount of free time in the afternoon. Each of us has to figure out a way of making space for the second period, which could be a little shorter because of its difficulty. The earlier you can practice the prayer in the morning, the better it usually goes. Let it be the first thing you undertake after washing up or having a cup of tea or coffee. Do it before you look at the paper, take a phone call, and especially before turning on the TV or checking your e-mail.

Maintaining external silence provides a context for the interior silence of not thinking about any particular issue. External silence is a stepping-stone to contemplative prayer and to that presence that has different levels of intensity, all the way up to experiencing the glory of God (God's presence within). The latter is what *contemplative* prayer in the full sense of the word is—an interpenetration of spirits that is more intimate than any other human experience. Contemplation has its own agenda, and so it is not something we can control. By repeatedly cultivating interior silence in formal prayer and attentiveness to God's presence in our activities, moments of union will begin to pop up in daily life spontaneously.

A very important aspect of contemplative prayer is that it does not fully do its job unless we are also working on our shadow side: that is, unloading the undigested material of our psychological unconscious. Some people may be held back in their progress if they make the prayer an end in itself. Practicing the regular periods of centering prayer and then allowing the gifts that we have received to be challenged—sometimes head on—by the reality of our community, other people, circumstances, the news of the day, opposition, financial worries, or personal illness: all of these are necessary aspects of the spiritual journey and are not obstacles. It is *our attitude toward them* that has to change. Contemplation, cultivated by the regular practice of centering prayer, provides the interior freedom to allow God to change us. Those who have been doing this practice for five or ten years may think of lengthening their ordinary period of centering prayer, as mentioned above.

Remember that contemplative prayer, especially when you up the time to forty minutes twice a day, and especially if you can manage an hour twice a day, is a good practice for those in a leadership role of any kind. The length of time provides you with the space to access the unconscious motivation that arises out of your instinctual needs. This is the most transformative kind of combination. You cultivate interior silence in prayer and you face the ruthless challenges of everyday life. As the presence of God infuses itself into your consciousness, you have an increased capacity to trust God and to let go of your attachments. By letting go I don't mean that you no longer feel the same old difficulties, or that your temperament or cultural baggage suddenly goes away. What I mean is: the difficulties do not have the same dominating effect they had in earlier periods of your spiritual journey. Your false self is being undermined and gradually dismantled by your two-fold practice. Feelings in response to emotional situations like disappointments and the frustration of worldly desires are still alive. The yearning for God has no limits, but every other desire needs to be moderated or, better, relinquished.

Meanwhile, the divine action in daily life and prayer is working with incredible wisdom. It provides us with the same situations over and over again, until we are completely detached all the way down to the soles of our feet. We can postpone this process by disregarding it, but the vocation we have and which we are trying to transmit to others is a desire for a state of mind that does not get discouraged by difficulties. It allows the Spirit to join us in our difficulties, which is a much greater grace than for the Spirit to take them all away. This life is not heaven. If it were, we might as well die and get a better slice of it. We seem to be caught up in an adventure in which God wants to feel what it is like to be human in each of us. That is a kind of knowledge that God has never had. Our gift is to provide him with our humanity in which the mysteries of Christ's life can be manifested again and again according to his will.

This is a key aspect of the contemplative movement toward transformation in Christ. God manifested is the God we know in ritual, sacrament, scripture, *lectio divina*, and in generous service to others: in short, in showing compassion and exercising the works of mercy. It is not doing everything, but doing what we can do in the light of our talents and duties in life. It is offering ourselves as a living cell to the Body of Christ and to contribute to the health of the particular organ or system that we are called to build up.

There is another aspect to God's presence that is incomparable, which is the unmanifest or uncreated. This is communion with the presence of God *as he is in himself* and which only pure faith can access. Such communion is vastly more significant than the awareness or experience of God that our faculties can relate to, whether they involve the overflow of the Spirit into the senses, the exercise of intellect, or the experience of the intuitive faculties. Saint Paul calls it the vision of God; that is to say, presence to presence—our basic being just as we are and God's being just as God is, without the intermediary of thoughts, feelings, or anything else. Through contemplative prayer a certain detachment from these experiences enables us to realize that we are *always* in contact with the unmanifest God that penetrates all things.

In this sense, there is no place to go to find him, and there is no place not to go. God is. He doesn't have to do anything; he just is. God, you might say, is not a noun, but a verb. He is always happening, and that happening is the content of the present moment, whatever that is. On our part, it means a willingness to live in the present moment without being attached to its content and without giving way to an aversion for it. This is learning the divine way to be human, which is what the Fathers of the Church called *deification*.

Paul says that we have within us the seed of God so that we are God's children and not just adopted (see 1 Corinthians 3:6). The seed of a parent is what passes on the particular DNA that we have. The Spirit is the divine DNA, so to speak, that truly makes us a participator in the divine life. The largess or generosity of God is the hospitality in which he invites us into the Trinitarian life itself!

One of the aspects of living in the present moment is to be in touch with one's personal history without remembering past experiences in a particular way. The past remains in us, but as part of the present moment and what we bring to the present moment, but it has no real existence apart from that.

It is usually not helpful to want to repeat some spiritual experience that was very meaningful to us ten or twenty years ago. It has been integrated into our spiritual journey. We can never reproduce exactly what happened, however much we may want to.

From this perspective, you can see how leadership is an ambiguous term in the Christian situation, where everyone is basically equal at the most fundamental level, which is the essence of our being. Everybody is designed to assist everybody else, so that whatever anybody else possesses is ours as well as theirs, and whatever we have is not just ours, but theirs. Moreover, whatever goodness we have has been given to us for the building up of the corporate human adventure, which scripture describes as the full age of Christ, or the *pleroma*.

In dealing with new people we are dealing with ourselves, or an aspect of ourselves sometimes revealed to us through our reactions to them, and by their different perspectives on many issues, cultural and otherwise. New people can broaden our perspectives. Leadership is in itself an enriching experience provided we are not unduly attached to it or think of it as something that we are doing all by ourselves. This is where opposition, even persecution, comes in handy.

Such trials invite us to move to a new level of letting go every time we pass through a difficult period. God does not will useless suffering. If you have gone through certain negative experiences, they will not be repeated. The fact that the same syndrome is repeated is a sign that we have not quite relinquished negative memories or habits lingering in our unconscious. To be *willing* to let go of them is all that is required. We cannot fix ourselves. It is in turning our life over completely to God that we allow him to heal the wounds of a lifetime.

Paul's teaching of the Mystical Body of Christ and the way he develops it through the human paradigm of growing up means that though we pass through infancy, adolescence, young adulthood, and old age, we imitate the way that nature works in our human development. From this perspective, any progress in becoming fully human is also spiritual progress. And as this continues, our particular gifts become more apparent. Sometimes certain charisms arise when these gifts are fully matured. Maybe you have not even noticed them yet. To your great surprise, you may find yourself saying or doing things that are beyond your own recognized limitations up until that moment.

When we experience an insight into our shadow side, an attachment that comes from earliest childhood, or an overidentification with our group or culture, this is truly a moment of growth if we can accept the insight. We have the capacity to accept this humiliating fact about our secret motivation and about our actions that we never really saw before. Maybe our friends or relatives noticed it, but we never quite owned up to the full depth of our human infirmities. Letting go opens space inside of us for the desire for God to emerge into our awareness. This is *contemplation* in the traditional Christian sense of the word. We do not complete the purification of the unconscious just from the prayer itself but *through both the prayer and the bringing of its fruits into daily life.* Divine love has to be manifested as well as experienced.

When you visit a foreign country to teach, you are speaking to people who have been moved to hear you or to come to a particular program. You can rely on this movement of God in them. You do not have to create the interest. It is already there or they would not have come. They have the innate capacity to respond, but they have, like we had, all kinds of obstacles in the way, such as preoccupations and attachments. If you let go of attachments that are excessive, you are liberated from the *domination* of that feeling as a preoccupation that lingers and creates moods, distress, frustration, and anxiety, and that may set off other afflictive emotions such as fear, anger, guilt, or shame. All of these faults serve the purpose of self-knowledge, but they are not meant to dominate or discourage. Once you acknowledge the feeling, relinquish it. By letting it go, your hands are open for the next inspiration, without lingering over an event that is now in the past.━►

# 3

## THE EXPERIENCE OF CENTERING PRAYER

LET US TAKE a look at our daily and expanding experience of centering prayer. As we progress, we are prepared to jettison everything in us that is an attachment, especially any unwillingness to acknowledge a particular weakness that we never noticed before. We also become aware that we are not our thoughts and we are not our feelings. We simply have them, and by accepting and releasing them, we are being liberated of our faults so that we can experience our inmost nature as the image and likeness of God. This we might call our True Self.

The primary discipline of centering prayer is letting go of all kinds of thoughts. Their disposal is not like putting junk in a wastebasket or garbage can. Rather, we are giving God our weaknesses by the simplest of gestures. As this process continues, it becomes an abiding disposition. Our human weakness and its consequences—such as compulsions, neurotic tendencies, and even mental disabilities—are not obstacles as long as we keep turning them over to God. Our growth in poverty of spirit enables the unmanifest character of God to reveal itself. They are problems for us but do not worry God. They are disturbing to us because we are preoccupied with ourselves instead of with God.

The secrecy that Jesus recommends in prayer is a mysterious yet very profound invitation. If we accept and consent, anything we are preoccupied with personally or socially is left behind as we sit down and introduce the sacred symbol of our will's consent to God's presence and action. We are often beset by our habitual interior dialogue, which is the endless conversation we have with ourselves. We keep letting go of every particular thought, feeling, memory, plan, judgment, evaluation, and even spiritual experiences, including the pervasive experience of peace.

All these are particular perceptions that are part of the interior dialogue that subtly supports the existence of the false self. The latter is our basic illusion. The false self is something we created, not God. When these three things— letting go of thoughts, turning ourselves completely over to God, and consenting to his presence and action within— become habitual dispositions, the transformation of consciousness begins to take place.

Contemplation is the growing presence of God as unlimited and undifferentiated. Without denying Christ's sacred humanity, we recognize it for the marvel that it is: the Word of God made flesh. The undifferentiated presence of God is the emergence of Christian contemplation, called by many mystics as the birth of the Word of God in our souls. We begin to vibrate with his immense energy. The Word of God is the ultimate source of everything that exists. In this perspective, external reality is just a particular set of vibrations that manifest God in various ways. Every creature and every activity are somehow contained or made possible by the Eternal Word.

The prayer in secret that Jesus refers to in Matthew 6:6 is the hiddenness of the unmanifest God, who can only be accessed by pure faith and not by our other human faculties. This is perhaps the meaning of the wrestling with God that Jacob endured (see Genesis 32:22–31). What were Jacob and the angel wrestling about? It seems to have something to do with whether or not Jacob would surrender himself completely to God. To call it a wrestling match seems like an accurate description.

Another image in Christian mysticism with deep roots in the Hebrew Bible is Elijah's experience on top of Mount Horeb. He discovered that God was not in the grandiose events that attracted his attention. God was "the sound of sheer silence" (1 Kings 19:12). To call sheer silence a sound is of course a paradox. What we are listening to in the centering prayer practice is the Mystery that is both in and beyond everything that exists. The proper response to this reality is gratitude and self-surrender.

At the same time, "in the sound of sheer silence," the Spirit brings to our attention our negative memories, habits, compulsions, and attitudes that constitute our personal slice of the human condition.

Contemplation was never easily accessible in any kind of lifestyle, especially in the lives of laypersons who have to spend most of their time trying to survive. If you are hungry and cold, you have to do something about it; simply to exist in this world requires an enormous amount of attention. We have to build with God's help an interior environment that can enable us to be totally present to events and to the persons whom we are with, and at the same time present to the deeper Source of our energy and intuitive consciousness.

A servant-leader is somebody in the Contemplative Outreach community who is beginning to recognize that he or she is a channel or instrument of God, and that whatever she or he has to offer is coming from God as sheer gift. Many texts in the New Testament are extremely profound and challenging, and it is not easy to explain what they mean in communicating them to others. Our presentations will go right over the heads of people unless they have already had a taste of contemplative prayer. At the same time, we should not presume that they have not had some experience of it, because there are probably thousands of people who are very advanced through the suffering, tragedy, and persecution they have undergone. They often react spontaneously in circumstances without even thinking about the heroic nature of their response.

Jean Vanier, the founder of L'Arche, writes about a Hindu lady whom he met in a hovel in a slum in India. It was obvious that the family was on the verge of starvation. He had a little money, which he donated to the mother. She immediately went to her neighbor and gave her half. He was blown away by her generosity. When she came back, he could not resist asking her: "How could you give so much away to your neighbor? You and your children are starving." She replied without a moment's hesitation: "They are hungry, too." This woman was manifesting her intuitive awareness of the oneness of the human family. We are most united with others in the experience of our common needs and weaknesses.

Scripture emphasizes the unity of the human family. Everybody, according to Genesis, is descended from our first parents. Scripture is not about teaching us history or science, but about the revelation of important spiritual truths in the form of stories that people at the time of its writing could understand. The oneness of humanity was intuited in a special way by the major prophets of Israel. They progressively perceived how equality with other human beings had to be a part of the human response to every aspect of human interaction.

As we have seen in Saint Paul's first letter to the Corinthians, the human body is a paradigm of this oneness. Through this example we can understand why what happens to other people touches us so deeply.

Thus, what we do for others we are doing for ourselves. In the Body of Christ everyone is accountable for everyone else. Human cultures usually build on previous cultures. There is an obvious continuity from family to tribe, from tribe to clan, from clan to village, from village to city-state, and then to nation. Science is reinforcing the oneness of the subatomic world that DNA establishes in the human body. In serving others we are serving the whole Body of Christ and building up this transformative milieu so that some day justice and peace can be accessible as a common and universal experience. Racial and nationalistic loyalties have to be relativized.

When you are familiar with the silence of centering prayer and awaken to your own inner resources, or lack thereof, your capacity to reach other people at the deepest level increases. They are experiencing substantially the same things as you are, but by means of their particular set of inner tapes or cultural conditioning. The experience that most unites human beings is the sense of our own inner self to the point of destitution.

Not knowing where happiness is to be found and being completely orientated by nature to finding it creates an immense dilemma. The apparent contradiction gives rise to a sense of confusion, alienation, loneliness, and not knowing where to go to find security, genuine caring, and acceptance. Only God can heal these states through the reassurance that comes in deep prayer and the experience of the Father whom Jesus calls "Daddy" (Abba).

To bring the sense of unity to our role of leadership is to recognize that we are not doing anything special, but only offering the healing remedy we have freely received. Our contribution, whatever that might be, is coming from God in us rather than from ourselves. It should not be a source of worry if nobody listens to our message. If a group disintegrates, that is God's problem. We are only serving his purposes, using what human means we can, without depending on them or ourselves to accomplish the spiritual work of transmitting the experience of God's love to the human family.

In *The Human Condition* I wrote that the question for the first half of life is, *"Where* are you?" Which means, "Where are you in your relationship with God?" The second half of life focuses on the question, *"Who* are you?" Once you find out where you are and what your relationship with God is, the second question spontaneously arises. There is no immediate answer to this second question in this life, and for that reason we feel lonely, isolated, and incomplete. Faith suggest that we are in fact complete and never separated from God, but we just have not found it out yet. We have not awakened to the loving presence of God within us that is forever waiting to be discovered.

In this perspective, the primary gift we can give to one another is to practice centering prayer faithfully and allow circumstances to refine the experience of peace that occurs. The abiding state of peace that God calls us to in the Beatitudes maintains it in daily life. Life happens. God works with our willingness and consent to bring about the transformation of our inmost being into the eternal happiness for which we have been created.

When you try to speak about the contemplative experience to people who have not had some taste of it, as we saw, they do not know what you are talking about; they usually change the subject. I do not think that somebody who has not had some experience of contemplative prayer can truly represent who he or she is. For example, the way we answer a letter, speak on the phone, what books we suggest others to read, communicate our deepest self. For words to be effective, they normally come out of a perspective based on one's own experience.

Our movement depends on experienced and advancing practitioners. After functioning as a network since 1984, we observe that the chapters that are most effective are those where there are hands-on and experienced people on the leadership teams. Where there have not been such people, the group has had to struggle. In other words, the kind of ministry that we are communicating normally needs a human face and human hands. It will be most accessible if you can find persons who have the experience that qualify them through contemplative practice and who can give full time to this ministry. For people living in the world, such commitment of time is not always possible. We can only accept as a gift whatever is left over from their family and other obligations.

It would be ideal if chapters could have a gathering place where they could offer hospitality as well as formation programs. Making friends with members of prayer groups and praying with them develop a sense of belonging. A place where practitioners of centering prayer could meet and pray on a regular basis and where new people can drop in could be a storefront or the basement of a church. It is in live communication that most things take place for us.➤

# PART II

CONSENTING
TO
SELF-SURRENDER

*The theme in 2008 was the willingness to let go of our vision, our projects, and what we most love for the love of God. As the spiritual journey matures, God invites us to consent to more radical forms of detachment. Our willingness to let go of plans, projects, and even of those dearest to us will occasionally be asked of us as ways of deepening our faith and love, and growing in our dependence on God alone.*

4

# THE SHATTERING OF OUR VISION

WHAT HAS BEEN discovered in recent research into scripture is that the Infancy Narratives are designed as a catechesis for new Christians, especially Jewish Christians. The Gospel of Matthew begins with a genealogy characteristic of the Hebrew Bible. One of the interests for us in the ancestry of Jesus is the fact that some of them were fairly disreputable folks.

Matthew is writing in about 80 C.E., forty years after the events of Jesus's life. He writes for a community of Jews who had become Christians and who were being persecuted by fellow Jews who were not Christians.

There is a pastoral concern in Matthew in his efforts to reassure his Jewish Christian colleagues that it was permissible to set aside the Mosaic law and to accept Saint Paul's view that it was not in force for baptized Christians (see Galatians 3:28). This would obviously evoke consternation and defensive measures from the Jewish community who had become Christians but who had remained faithful to their previous religious commitments and practices.

John's gospel has clearly a catechetical purpose. It is trying to understand the mystery of Christ and the meaning of the redemption, especially the passion, death, and resurrection of Jesus. Luke's gospel seems to be a catechetical instruction aimed at Gentiles who did not have to deal with memories of the Mosaic law. For that gospel, Mary is the model for newly baptized Christians.

The good news of the Gospel is great news indeed, but how do you live this out in a world where there is much opposition, and in the case of those Christians that Matthew was concerned about, persecution?

Matthew's catechetical model is Joseph, the husband of Mary. When we look at the Infancy Narratives, we are not concerned primarily with history, though certain events were known about Jesus's early life. They are arranged in such a way as to encourage readers or hearers of the Christian belief system and practice in the face of misunderstanding and rejection from their ethnic and religious contemporaries.

Matthew's gospel is addressing the question of how to be a Christian when people are not treating you decently or quite the reverse. He is responding to the issue: "Shouldn't the Good News protect us from the invasion of persecution and the ups and downs of daily life with all its banality, not to mention the humiliation of our own personal failures?"

The second question that may arise is, "What has the Good News actually done for us in the concrete? How does it teach us to live ordinary life with peace and joy? How can we lead a life committed to the imitation of Christ? If Jesus invites everyone to follow Him, where is he going?" The road to Jerusalem is clearly the direction he is taking, but this is not a path that sounds like good news when you add Calvary and the Cross to his trip.

The proclamation that the apostles are preaching *is* good news. We need models. Matthew and Luke provide us with Joseph and Mary respectively.

What is Mary's role as a model of the Good News? Her role is to show what it means to be incarnations of Christ. She is mother of the Word made flesh, and each of us, according to the Gospel, is invited to become a child of God, too. To let Christ be born in us is the bottom line of Luke's Christmas proclamation.

The light of Christmas according to Luke is the realization that Christ is eager to be born in us, and that similar situations are going to happen in our lives that occurred in his earthly life and in Mary's. We are to incarnate Christ in our daily lives in spite of the obstacles that surround us. Christians then should not be surprised at being opposed or even persecuted by their compatriots, relatives, and friends.

Let us look at Joseph as presented by Matthew as a model of what the Christian life can do for us and expects of us. His example is a strong incentive to allow the same process to occur in us that occurred in his experience. It is not easy to live as Joseph did. It is not his actions so much as his attitude of total surrender and trust that emerges in his various trials. His path is the assimilation of the passion and death of Jesus with its depth of meaning. It is also an invitation to glorify God in our own bodies and growing-up experiences by letting Christ be born in our specific situation, with all our personal limitations, social difficulties, and the persecutions that may arise.

The following of Christ is thus not a magic carpet to bliss! It does not assure us of wealth and security. It does not promise us a ripe old age. It does not provide us with fame and fortune, power and control over others, and what is even more significant, it does not provide us with the power to control ourselves.

That last point is an important issue. The process in which Christ is born in us and transforms us into citizens of the Kingdom is a state of consciousness rather than a place. It is not *any* state of consciousness, but *Christ's consciousness of the Father as Abba*. There the Good News reveals the extraordinary beauty and depth of God's invitation and challenge to become divine. God is not just transcendent, or the God of Israel, or the God of armies, but our Abba, our loving Father, the God of infinite mercy.

Here we need to look at the broader context of the human family. Where did it come from? Where is it going?

Is it a species that started out in paradise with Adam and Eve, or is it rather a species that is evolving, the chief of whose problems is rooted in the fact that it has not become fully human yet, let alone divine? God knows each member of the human family through and through with the loving concern of the most caring of parents—an idea more or less contained in the relationship that Jesus had with the Ultimate Reality as Abba. This term was unheard of in religious circles in his time. God is close, tender, motherly, and all the other attributes that go with this homey Aramaic word for *father*. This is the revolutionary attitude toward the Ultimate Reality that Jesus communicated to his contemporaries and is trying to do for us.

All that Jesus teaches about his Father does not change the human condition from its powerlessness and confusion, its ignorance and darkness, and its dependency on animal and neurological networks that exist in our tripartite brain. Our problem is that we have not integrated the lower instincts of our nature that are rooted in our animal ancestry. We are confronted with the struggle to be fully human when we still have all the neurology to enable us to live in this world as thinking animals.

Modern research has made clear that it is not only our developmental behaviors from early childhood that separate us from the divine experience. The physiology of the brain depends on habits entrenched from earliest childhood. The instinctual needs of human nature are not just ideas, but physical constructs in which the brain reacts to the external stimuli of the senses through electrical currents and translates them, not as we would like, but with the same habitual reactions we have experienced in the past.

When we try to change an emotional pattern or behavior, we need to be aware that the brain is set up to do its own thing, which is to send the energy down the same old channels that were dug in early childhood. Our first job is to get a bulldozer, so to speak, and flatten the playing field. A bulldozer unfortunately does not fit into the brain! Thus, to change the way that we react to things emotionally, mentally, and sociologically is a massive and lengthy undertaking.

We still do not know how the collective unconscious affects our behavior, especially how our genetic DNA determines in some degree who we are. We are in an interior place where we can no longer return to the freedom from responsibility of the animals from which we evolved, and we cannot ascend into fully human behavior, and still less that of the Kingdom of Heaven.

The cross is a striking image of human nature as unevolved and locked into our present stage of consciousness, which is neither that of an animal nor an angel. We are in fact *crucified* between heaven and earth. Hence the need for Christ, the divine human person, to reveal to us the human situation that we are immersed in, which he took completely to himself in his incarnation and redeemed on the cross.

The Good News of the Gospel is in a reality that involves a certain amount of bad news. But it is not news to God. He is fully aware of the evolutionary process and is probably less concerned about our inevitable faults than we are. If we are unevolved, God would hardly expect us to behave like angels or even as mature human beings.

We find ourselves with the clear call from the Gospel to become divine by participation, which is what grace is. Matthew has chosen Joseph as a model of how we may expect the Good News to work itself out in our lives, and how to respond to the ultimate conundrum that we experience, which theology calls the consequences of original sin. We are born and brought up without the experience of God while possessing at the same time the destiny of a creature designed for boundless happiness. Our desire for happiness, which is probably the greatest proof of God's presence in us, has been inserted into the most unlikely candidates that anyone could possibly imagine.

God seems to have chosen the least of all intellectual creatures for the major manifestation of his inmost being. Perhaps there are many other worlds that will be discovered in time. Why should this be the only universe when we believe that God is infinite? In any case, it is the only one we know, and hence this is the one that is the primary focus of revelation.

The basic question that everybody has as a partner in the drama of human life is how matter—what seems to be the very opposite of all that we mean by God—is destined to become divine in us, a project that truly no one but God could possibly have thought up.

Our destiny is God's own infinite happiness. We are meant to participate in it, but the path to it involves first the experience of our powerlessness to achieve it by ourselves. This is one of the biggest of all the issues of our spiritual life: how to be peaceful with this situation. We possess almost infinite aspirations in a body, soul, and consciousness that make us aware that we cannot possibly gain peace and happiness under our own power. In fact, we tend to resist God's efforts to provide us with the attitudes that would be most helpful in achieving it.

So, we need models, and Luke and Matthew present Mary and Joseph respectively, given the population that they are addressing, as manifesting the necessary dispositions and behaviors to experience full human happiness. Let us first take a look at the catechesis in Matthew: "Now the birth of Jesus the Messiah took place in this way. When his mother Mary had been engaged to Joseph, but before they lived together, she was found to be with child from the Holy Spirit" (1:18). We are familiar with the Annunciation and Mary's consent after her initial hesitation (see Luke 1:26–38). Her hesitation was well-founded. We can only guess about what this meant for her and her family.

The Jewish custom at the time, according to many exegetes, consisted in a couple being formally married, but not living together for a certain time. Custom required that the bride stay in her own home for several months. Then she would move to the home of her husband and the marriage was consummated. Until that time sexual relations were not to take place.

This means that Joseph was thrust by the angel's announcement into an enormous and harrowing double bind. Joseph became aware of Mary's pregnancy, knowing that he was not the biological father. To read more of the passage: "Her husband, Joseph, being a righteous man . . ." (Matthew 1:19). The term *righteous* is a key word in the Hebrew vocabulary. It means he fulfilled the Law and was dedicated to it.

The text continues: "and unwilling to expose her." The law required that an unfaithful wife be divorced, and so he decided "to dismiss [divorce] her quietly." How quietly can you divorce someone in a small town, especially in the town of Nazareth, "the place out of which no good came" (John 1:46)? Joseph decided to divorce her secretly and not to make a public statement of her seeming misbehavior. The fact that she was pregnant could mean either that Joseph was not a righteous man and had sexual relations with her contrary to the accepted custom, or that she was an adulteress. Adulteresses could be stoned to death, as we learn in John's gospel. People took sexual misbehavior very seriously in the Hebrew community.

Mary was about fifteen years old at this point. We don't know whether she told Joseph the actual story. If you were pregnant by the Holy Spirit, would you be inclined to tell somebody? The chances are good that Mary kept quiet. One reasonably suspects this might have been a motive in leaving her family under the guise of visiting Elizabeth. Elizabeth was also pregnant in an extraordinary way, but not as extraordinary as Mary's. In any case, Mary left the public eye and went to spend three or four months with Elizabeth in seclusion.

What must have been her concern and angst to be carrying the Holy One, given Hebrew understanding, and not being able to tell anyone about it, and wondering what in the world Joseph might be thinking of her! She evidently did not tell him. It would probably have made the situation even more difficult for him.

Joseph, in the light of the unfolding situation, had to take some action. As a righteous person, he could not compromise his own integrity, and commitment to the common good. To human eyes, Mary must have had relations with someone; otherwise this baby would not be appearing in her body. On the other hand, Joseph had to contend with his immense love for her and his appreciation of her extraordinary spiritual qualities. She represented his best hope and dearest vision for his own personal happiness.

If we take her conversation with the angel into account, Mary implies that she and Joseph had an agreement to live as brother and sister, which would enable her to remain a virgin. Still, we do not know for sure just what revelation the sacred authors are trying to give of her situation. What seems clear is that Joseph was trying to follow the general custom, while at the same time his love of Mary could not envisage risking her being stoned or humiliated. If he took her into his home before the customary delay, it would be perceived or presumed that he was the father. He would no longer be the righteous man that people thought he was.

He went through a period of inner searching, no doubt in a state of deep anguish. One could hardly imagine a marriage with more difficulties surrounding it than this one! It is also possible, as some authors have suggested, that he suspected the Mystery that had taken up residence in her. Jewish people were expecting the Messiah to be born at any time, and most Jewish maidens we are told would have been happy to be his chosen mother.

If Joseph suspected the Mystery, he might have thought, "If she is the mother of the Messiah, this is not the place for me." In any case, he had to decide what to do to protect her reputation while submitting to the accepted social custom, now complicated by his suspicion of a transcendent presence within her that he did not feel worthy to be involved in.

The traditional ideas of Mary's perpetual virginity makes one wonder what kind of an agreement they had prior to the coming of the angel to Mary. Clearly, his plans were completely upset and negated by her mysterious pregnancy. He could not believe that it was due to another man. . . . But, how else could it have come about? He had no answer.

This great God of ours, as Jesus has revealed him, does not feel bound by his own rules. Thus, what you least expect to happen happens, and what you expect to happen doesn't. This divine pattern of action warns us not to judge Joseph or anyone else, including external behaviors that seem to be inappropriate. Only God knows all the facts. His database has information that we do not possess. Nobody but him knows all the factors that influenced us in early life. We know that there is a certain window of freedom of choice in our decisions and behaviors, and that this measure of freedom is the specific human predicament. Animals, vegetables, and other forms of life do not have this problem. Humans are greatly influenced by secondary causes like social events, other people, and emotional or mental problems, but our actual accountability in a particular choice is God's secret.

Each of us carries the burden, sometimes very heavy, of our ancestry, our social milieu, and their influences on us from the time of our conception. God knows exactly what these are. He loves us just as we are, and because of his infinite compassion, our weakness seems to be especially attractive to him. To repeat once again what has already been said, the most basic human double bind consists of having the transcendent destiny of boundless happiness as a sharer in God's divine life, and at the same time the awareness of the impossibility of reaching it under our own strength. The good news is that there is a way to deal with this dilemma. That path is modeled by Joseph and Mary, each in their own way. Basically, it consists of being content for love of God to live with our external difficulties, endless faults, and overwhelming weaknesses that constitute our particular slice of the human condition.

Not knowing where true happiness is to be found is called *illusion* in most of the world religions. Concupiscence or craving is looking for that happiness in the wrong places. God's grace gives us the ever-deepening conviction that even if we knew where true happiness is to be found, we are utterly incapable of pursuing it on our own strength. We are thus completely dependent on God's mercy.

Is this a disaster? This is actually the first Beatitude in the Sermon on the Mount (see Matthew 5:3). The Fruits of the Spirit and the Beatitudes that come from the Seven Gifts of the Spirit are participations in the mind and heart of Christ, communicated to us in virtue of his transmission of the Kingdom of God through scripture, the sacraments, and our acceptance of God's will for us. The beauty of the first Beatitude is its sense of complete dependence on God. It is a growing awareness of our personal spiritual destitution, without being upset by it or disturbed: it is contentment to be powerless and, at the same time, totally dependent on God to prepare us for participating in the divine life.

### The Example of Jesus

Jesus said to his disciples, "Come follow me." Where is he going? Not just to Jerusalem and to the cross where he experienced spiritual poverty and the whole gamut of the human weakness, but even more profoundly, when the sins of the world fell upon him as indicated in the words of Paul: "For our sake he made him to be sin who knew no sin" (2 Corinthians 5:21).

The key to the understanding of the heart of Christ is his consent to be emptied of his divine privileges and to be identified with the full consequences of deliberate sin, even to the point of feeling abandoned by the Father. In his case, as the Word of God made flesh, he "did not regard equality with God as something to be exploited, but emptied himself" (Philippians 2:6–7).

*Kenosis* is the Greek word for *emptying*. In applying it to ourselves, it means the emptying of our false selves so that the divine activity may enter into us just as we are. Christ emptied himself of his divinity so that he could become totally vulnerable as a human being like we are. This is the "admirable exchange" that the Christmas liturgy celebrates: that is, the exchange of human weakness for the strength and power of God. Christ has emptied himself of the divine privileges in order to share the human condition, even to becoming the last and least of all humanity. Through his resurrection, we are introduced and thrust into the divine life and love.

What was the motive behind this divine activity? What is it revealing about God? The purpose of Christ's incarnation, as he said, is primarily to reveal the Father. There is no self as we know it in God. The primary and eternal activity of the Trinity is the total emptying of each of the three divine relationships into the others. The Godhead is the flow of self-sacrificing love from one divine person to the others. We are invited to immerse ourselves in that flow of selfless love, into the stream of charity that throbs within the Trinitarian relationships, and which enters the human condition through Christ's incarnation.

Joseph, as a major figure in the actual redemptive Mystery, is obviously caught up in this dynamic of emptying. In the Godhead, total sacrifice is absolute joy and delight, but in human affairs, where there is a certain freedom, sacrifice normally involves immense suffering. To surrender ourselves as completely as the divine persons freely give themselves to each other is the divine invitation, spoken to us from the cross. In this perspective, sacrifice is the ultimate meaning of the universe. The example of Jesus is the divine way of being human. It is the ultimate evolution of life from its lowest or most primitive forms, into the highest state of consciousness that is possible for human beings.

In the midst of Joseph's enormous double bind, the angel says to him, "Do not be afraid to take Mary as your wife." Those words imply that he was indeed afraid of the divine Mystery that had taken possession of her. Maybe the angel was confirming his suspicions, as if to say, "You are right. But you are wrong in staying away from the mystery, because even though you are not worthy, you are the person God has chosen."

God does not seem to pay much attention to worthiness. In fact, he seems to prefer to perform his greatest works through the most inappropriate instruments, including the weakest, most unlikely people.

Saint Thérèse of Lisieux, perhaps the greatest contemplative of our time, recovered and renewed the contemplative dimension of the Gospel for contemporary Christianity. In her writings she says that if God could find a soul that was weaker than hers, he would fill it with even greater graces than she had received, if it abandoned itself completely to him.

God does not need our accomplishments or our talents. The angels are much better equipped with all that stuff. Again, an observation by Saint Thérèse reveals that what God needs from us is almost unbelievable. If we could accept it, it would save us a lot of trouble, especially if we learned to do it early in life. What God most wants from us is to *allow him to love us.*

To be loved by infinite love can involve complications. It teaches that *being* is more important than *doing.* This is a basic contemplative disposition. In other words, receiving is greater than giving. That seems to contradict the statement of Saint Paul in which he claims that "it is better to give than to receive" (Acts 20:35). But that advice refers to the beginning stages of the spiritual life.

The love of our own spiritual poverty is one of the greatest of God's gifts. We can only learn this by the loss of the false self. What the world needs is people of great vision like Joseph, because vision gives meaning and significance to an everyday life that often seems aimless, fruitless, and frittered away in trivialities.

Virginity primarily means humility in the scriptures. It is Mary's humility that makes her incomparable in the use of her own personal freedom from a false self. We celebrate this revelation as part of the teaching that the Immaculate Conception implies. She never had to deal with the particular problem of a false self. She did, however, have to deal with the ordinary rough and tumble of daily life, especially as the spouse of Joseph, who must have been very happy to take Mary into his home.

Recently, exegetes have made another interesting discovery regarding Jewish custom at the time. When a child was born, the father did not own or take possession of the child without first stating publicly his intention to accept responsibility for it. Thus, a father did not have to accept responsibility. Joseph freely accepted Jesus and all the obligations of fatherhood that went with that acceptance. Joseph, as a righteous Jew, knew these had very serious consequences, economic as well as social.

Let us look at other significant points of Joseph's life experience. He had gone through an enormous conversion as the result of his double bind. I refer to his plan to live with

Mary and the contradiction her pregnancy introduced into the situation. Life with Mary was his primary vision. If he followed the Jewish custom, he also agreed to be the foster father of Jesus and his primary mentor. Those became his two great visions, the two eyes with which he saw reality.

The spiritual journey is often compared to a desert or ocean. The person who is negotiating this journey comes upon the equivalent of an oasis in a desert or a harbor in the ocean. The temptation is to think that the journey has come to an end and that all of one's immense efforts are finally producing the longed-for fruit, But the oasis or harbor can become a place of poison for someone who is in the transformative process. In the spiritual journey there are high levels of spiritual attainment, consolation, and enlightenment that invite one to settle down at that level and to consider it the end of the journey. Unless one pushes on, however, the journey can get stuck in what seems like spiritual accomplishment.

God gives us plenty of chances to let go of our vision, and more than that, often takes our vision and shatters it, especially if he sees that this is the only way in which the vision can actually *become* the vision, rather than just *thinking about* the vision.

Notice the emptying that takes place in being invited to let go of what is dearest to us. In the spiritual journey this could include our experience of God, which can be so rewarding that one would like to settle for that experience and not take further risks. It is essential to keep going. On the other hand, it is the *willingness* to allow one's vision to be shattered, not the actual giving it up, as we see in Joseph's case, that is necessary and liberating. Then God reaffirms Joseph's path. His attitude toward it has now completely changed. He is now carrying out the vision as the will of God rather than his own. He knows that God has chosen him for the ministry of caring for Mary and Jesus, and he wholeheartedly consents.

Now watch the way God works with the new Joseph, whose journey has vastly matured by his experience of being ready and willing to give up his vision.

Giving up one's vision is not the end of the journey, but the beginning. The sense of a separate self also has to be worked on and emptied. Life then begins to challenge us to carry out what we committed ourselves to do.

The fact that God has called us does not mean the commitment is going to be easy or that we have adequately responded. All we have done may be to put a big toe on the path of following Christ. Life remains to be lived. Notice what it is for Joseph.

First of all, he could not provide the normal conditions for the birth of Mary's child. That must have been a blow to his ego, in a religion and society where fathers were supposed to be the head of the family. They were only considered righteous when they provided everything necessary for the family.

Shortly after Jesus's birth came his presentation in the Temple, as required by the Law. Simeon takes the child in his arms and says: "This child is destined for the falling and the rising of many in Israel" (Luke 2:34). Then Simeon says to Mary, "A sword will pierce your own soul, too" (v. 35). What happened to Joseph's soul when he heard those words?

Later, an angel appears in a dream and says, "Take the child and his mother, and flee to Egypt" (Matthew 2:13). The authorities are after him. So he has to escape to Egypt as a refugee. The fact that God has chosen us as he did Joseph does not mean that everything is going to be hunky-dory. On the contrary, life will call upon us to put into practice our commitment and the revised vision that we now identify with.

Mary, Joseph, and Jesus become refugees like so many people in our time. We do not know how they got to Egypt. It was a hazardous journey and they were unlikely to know anybody when they got there. Thus, they identified with the vast numbers of people through the ages who are exiles or refugees from various forms of injustice or human misery. That must have been a blow to Joseph's ego because, as a good Jewish father, he was expected to provide for his family at home.

In any case, when they returned from Egypt Joseph could not choose the place where it would be most appropriate for the family to live, but again had to hide from the authorities, who were still concerned about the boy king whom the Magi had spoken to them about. The Holy Family went to Nazareth, which as we have seen, was allegedly a place nobody would want to live. Thus, Joseph fails again. He does not seem to measure up to the cultural ideal of the righteous person and an exemplary father.

Much later, the boy Jesus decides to slip away and converse with the teachers in the Temple. A runaway child is a humiliation and an embarrassment for most parents. When Joseph and Mary finally find Jesus, he shows little interest in them. He asks, "Did you not know I must be in my Father's house?" (Luke 2:49). In this way, Jesus puts Joseph on notice that he does not regard him as his true father. Was it a rejection of the fatherhood of Joseph from Joseph's perspective? Or was this perhaps his crucifixion of heart, his loss not just of Mary, but of Jesus? In any case, it may have completed his spiritual journey. We do not hear about him after that incident.

It was about twenty years from that moment in the Temple until Jesus began his preaching career. Matthew's catechesis seems to warn that you are not going to be able to stay in the harbor or in any oasis you encounter on the journey. Life is going to return to the same question again and again, challenging what your vision of yourself is.

Joseph's vision happened to be: "Are you a righteous Jewish father?" His cultural conditioning would have said, "Yes, I am." But life was telling him, "No, you're not." Would he be willing to accept just to be himself and to deal with the increasing depth of his humiliation? In any case, every vision, however high, has to be shattered, whether it is our vision of the spiritual life, of the Church, of Jesus Christ, or even of God. Such is the traditional journey through the desert or through the sea.

To sum up, Joseph's greatest contribution to the transformation of the human family and its movement from biological to spiritual evolution—an enormous step in the understanding of God's plan for the universe—was his marriage to Mary. That marriage seems to change God's original commandment to Adam and Eve "to be fruitful and multiply, and fill the earth" (Genesis 1:28). Or rather it gives it a new dimension, a greater fulfillment. In the persons of Mary and Joseph, God seems to be challenging the human family to fill the Earth not in a quantitative manner but in a *qualitative* manner. This new dispensation is not to increase the number of people, but to increase and multiply *the experience of the full development of divine love*. The marriage of Mary and Joseph signifies this new understanding of human destiny, for it was not their physical joining together but *their spiritual love* that brought the Son of God into the world and created the milieu in which he grew to human maturity.➤

5

# The Sacrifice of What We Most Love

WE HAVE BEEN looking at Joseph as a model for catechumens regarding the Christian life and what it is like to live it. We saw that his crucial double bind was the loss of Mary when she became pregnant. Joseph found himself caught between exposing her or taking her into his home as his wife and losing his own reputation. A Jewish couple was not supposed to come together while they were living in separate houses, yet she was pregnant. This pregnancy to human eyes was either by him or she was an adulteress. He chose to shield Mary's reputation and to sacrifice his own.

The language of the text also suggests that he might have been worried about getting involved in a divine mystery that he did not understand and felt unworthy of. His other choice was to let her take the rap by divorcing her quietly and to maintain his righteous reputation. God, through the angel's message, was asking him to relinquish his own good name and to take her into his home, which meant, to the average experienced eye, that he had misbehaved in the engagement process. We are not told whether he ever recovered from that disgrace, at least in his own hometown.

Matthew's gospel was written for Jewish Christians, as we saw. Reading this text, they would notice the similarities with other persons identified in the Hebrew Bible. The friends of God are clearly marked for purification, to say the least. God is deeply involved in their transformative process. The process has certain distinct characteristics that are discernible.

Jewish converts to Christianity would be thinking about the covenants that God had made with a number of people before Jesus established the New Covenant. There were covenants with Adam and Eve, Noah, Melchizedek, Abraham, and Moses. The question arises, are these other covenants that preceded the New Covenant still in place? Some theologians think that whatever God agrees to, he does not ever rescind. If this is true, the Word of God has been active in the human population since its beginning. Rites that exist in other faiths, including nature religions, are salvific for them, and they may be the means by which God brings them to redemption. The documents of Vatican II (1962–1966) teach that Jesus and his redemptive activity are the ultimate source of everyone's salvation.

Abraham was called by God into a developing process. God promised him in his old age that he would beget a son through whom all nations would be blessed. Abraham is said to have put his faith in God, and God accounted it as righteousness for him (see Genesis 15:5–6).

Paul teaches that it is faith and not works that is salvific (see Romans 3:28). Notice the personal relationship that is implied. It is not a system or a series of beliefs that we accept, but rather the surrender of ourselves to the mystery of God's presence in every aspect of our lives.

Abraham's son Isaac was born to the surprise of everyone including his mother, Sarah. Isaac became the apple of Abraham's eye and the beloved child of his old age. Having shown Abraham all kinds of favors, material and spiritual, and providing him with a son when he was so advanced in years, God gave Abraham the command to sacrifice the boy on a mountain that he would show him. The text gives poignant details as Abraham obeys and takes his son Isaac on a three-day journey up a mountain with the young man carrying the wood for the sacrifice. They walked along in silence for a long time. Isaac finally asked, "Dad, here is the wood. Where is the sacrifice?" Abraham replied, "God will take care of that, my son" (Genesis 22:7–8).

When they reached the summit of the mountain, Abraham laid the boy on the pyre and prepared to slay him with his knife. As he was about to strike, at the very last moment, a ram appeared in the brush nearby, and an angel swooped down and cried out to Abraham, "Don't touch the boy!" A little later, God says to Abraham, "Because you have done this and not withheld your son . . . I will make your offspring as numerous as the stars of heaven and as the sand that is on the seashore" (22:17–18). We can almost hear gratitude and astonishment in God's voice as it is recorded in the text. Abraham was fully prepared to carry out God's will under the most difficult circumstances that could be imagined.

The sacrifice of Isaac has become a symbol of *the sacrifice of what we most love* for the greater love of God. These are the historic circumstances in which not only was Joseph, the husband of Mary, placed, but that occur again and again in our own lives. This is a pattern of self-surrender. It is not an abstract process, nor is it a heroic rising to the occasion to put up with some particular difficulty or trial. Rather, it is the classic human experience of love that is overwhelmingly precious, but which is terminated by death or rejection.

What we most love can be ourselves or another person. It could also be our job, our role, our nation, our spiritual reputation, or our accomplishments. In the religious life of the nineteenth century, one finds this happening almost regularly with the founders of the different orders. Many founders were thrown out or replaced by some ambitious person in their organization. One of the most famous of the victims was St. Francis of Assisi. He had ideas for the reformation of the Church, and he put his whole soul into establishing in the community he founded the simplicity of the Gospel. The Church authorities of the time did not show much interest. An institution tends to be slower than individuals in seeing the need for reform. In this case, the

Church in the person of the Pope would not approve the strictness of his rule with regard to absolute poverty. This enabled the intellectual side of the order to take over, and it was Brother Elias as superior general who eventually gave the Franciscan Order its final form, rejecting much of what Francis had hoped to accomplish for God and for the Church.

This development led to Francis's retirement into a hermitage where he entered a deep night of spirit culminating in receiving the stigmata. The goal he had invested everything in his whole life to accomplish was shattered.

The inevitable sacrifice of what we hoped for, often called our vision, is almost certainly going to be challenged in the course of time, and we may have to sacrifice our idea of what we thought God wanted of us. This happens to all of us in small matters as a preparation for bigger ones. It is God's response to the generosity that is willing to choose him over everything else. In the case of Joseph and Mary, Joseph was willing to send Mary away for the love of God in order to keep God's law. Once he made the inward sacrifice, as we saw, she was returned to him.

Thus, it is the *willingness* to let go of everything for God's sake that is required, not the actual fact of doing so. One's vision may actually be part of God's salvific plan. God was evidently thrilled with Abraham's fidelity and willingness to let go of his beloved son. The boy's continuing life, however, was the necessary means by which the promises of God to Abraham could be fulfilled.

When Abraham was told by God to sacrifice Isaac, did Abraham believe that God would raise Isaac from the dead? Abraham's conscience was faced by an overwhelming double bind: his very special and tender love for the son of his old age and God's order to sacrifice him.

Abraham's conscience seems to have been radically changed and liberated from the cultural conditioning of his times by means of this enormous trial. Perhaps on that long journey up the mountain, Abraham began to doubt the accepted practice of his time that condoned and even fostered human sacrifice. Did the God that he *knew* and whose friendship meant everything to him really require the sacrifice of his beloved son?

With this question growing in his mind, Abraham proceeded with the necessary preparations, even to the point of raising the knife in readiness to kill his beloved son. The angel then ordered him not to harm the boy. Abraham had already made the sacrifice of the one he loved most in the world by means of his total surrender to God's will as he understood it. Thus, Abraham was able to trust his personal *experience* of God, rejecting the full force of his cultural conditioning. God thus resolved Abraham's double bind, liberating him from the universally accepted practice of human sacrifice common to society of his time.

This dramatic near-tragedy makes clear that the sacrifice

of what we most love can never include human sacrifice, but leads to the total giving of *ourselves* to God. His witness brought to an end the custom of sacrificing a human being (or beings) for any reason and from every kind of scapegoating.

Abraham's poignant suffering can be transferred to the Blessed Mother who was fully aware of the angel's words that Jesus, her son, was to be the savior of the world (see Luke 1:33). How this was to be done was not explained to her. When she saw him dying on the cross, did she believe that God, the Father, would raise him from the dead? Daily life is meant to cultivate this attitude of willingness to let go of anything that we possess at God's request, including not only the people we most love, but also our own self-image and ego.

It is not that our objects of special love are wrong or sinful; it is rather that the love of God has greater plans for us than we can conceive of. Scripture has picked out models of the dispositions of Jesus for us to imitate. God lifts a corner of the veil hiding the Ultimate Mystery once we accept in faith that God is sheer self-surrender and love.

The Trinity is a mystery of a love that exceeds anything we can experience in this life, but which is the source of everything of value that we do know in this life. In the Trinity, the Father is eternally giving the totality of who he is to the Son. He is always begetting the Son along with everything that is included in the coming to actuality of the infinite potentialities that are present and lie hidden in the Father. If the Son receives everything and returns it to the Father, part of this return is to manifest the movement of the gift of divine love into human affairs. The expression of this sacrifice is Christ's humanity.

It is not our salvation that is uppermost in the mind of Jesus, but rather the revelation of the humility and love of the Father who gives everything to the Son. The Son returns the whole of the Godhead to the Father in the love of the Spirit, who reconstitutes them, so to speak, as they empty themselves of all that they are and receive it back again from each of the others. In God, knowledge is *being* the other. For God to know something is to *be* that thing, although not limited to any particular thing.

As we explore the depths of the Trinity, it begins to register on us that everything is in God because, in the ultimate sense, there is nothing else. God is everything. Hence by becoming no-thing ourselves, we become everything by participation. This spaciousness is characteristic of the experience of the ongoing stages of contemplation.

The humility of God is arresting. It is as if God *prefers not to be God*. In the Incarnation the eternal Word empties himself of the divine and becomes one with the lowest form of intelligent life that we know of in this universe. Further, it seems that God is not primarily interested in acts of gratitude or worship. These devotional practices are for our benefit. He only needs one thing: our willingness to be loved infinitely, not because we deserve it, but because of our desperate need and his infinite mercy.

What do we often do when God seems to treat us badly? We get angry and feel we are being treated unjustly. Job wanted to call God into some kind of heavenly court and prove himself innocent. A self-appointed group of comforters browbeat him with pious platitudes about suffering caused by sin, which was a popular notion of the time. Job would not accept their explanation because he knew he was innocent and because he was honest. He said so and defended himself. His relationship with God was shattered, but his relationship with God before his great trials began was based on his social and cultural conditioning, which did not understand the height, and length, and breadth and depth of the love of God and judged God's activity by human standards.

From the point of view of human justice, God seemed to be unjust to Job. In the first chapter of the book of Job, God affirms that Job is blameless, but Satan challenges him, saying, "He serves you only because you treat him so well. Just send him a few trials and see what you get in return," (see Job 1:10–11). God allows Satan to act.

God is using Satan's malice to bring Job to a new level of perception of what divinity is. He could not reach this relationship without the shattering of his idea of God, which limited him to a certain human standard of justice. People are still doing this. They say, "How can God treat me this way when I try to serve him? I work so hard in ministry of various kinds, keep all the commandments, go to church on Sunday, and live a life of continuous good works. I visit the homeless and teach centering prayer. And what do I get? The back of his hand!"

That is more or less what Job was feeling and verbalizing as he lost all his property, family, reputation, and bodily health. He even accuses God of being the murderer of the innocent. Finally, God appears to Job in a whirlwind and asks, "Where were you when I made the stars and the ocean and the animals?" (38:1, 4ff). At the end of God's speech, Job simply withdraws all his questions. The only answer to all the questions about God is God.

God is sheer love, but it is a love that is not sentimental. It is a love that is trying to share pure and unselfish love with these very human instruments who do not know their right hand from their left, yet have the destiny of participating in the divine life. Consent is the proper attitude and primary response to God, not some kind of action or accomplishment.

Consent is the heart of contemplative prayer and of the centering prayer method. Thus, when we sit down for centering prayer, we are actually consenting to God and allowing God to be God freely in us. This is the basic disposition for receiving the transmission of divine life mediated through Christ's redeeming activity. It is not limited to Christians because Christ's redeeming activity has been applied backwards and forwards in time to include every human being that ever existed. It is also available to everyone through a variety of channels outside of religion including nature, creativity, art, service to others, genuine science, conjugal love, and other ways. Religion remains, however, the best conveyor of divine life.

Abraham's willingness to surrender what he most loved at God's request enabled him to become the father of the Abrahamic religions: Islam, Judaism, and Christianity. What these religions essentially teach is *an acceptance of God as God* is. We allow him, through daily life and the unfolding of our lives, to bring us to an ever-deeper capacity to surrender who we think we are and to accept who we actually are.

Union with God involves the letting go of our self-image *as a fixed point of reference*. Jesus identified with the human condition and provided us with an example of how this relationship can be worked out in practice. The great figures of the Old and New Testament are examples of how it succeeded in human lives that were not completely possessed by the divine life. These people were just humans and showed us that it is possible for everyone to manifest the divine life in one's particular human nature.

By the repeated sacrifice of Isaac in our lives—what we most love—we gradually let go of our self-image and allow God to be God in us. We prepare for the self-surrender that culminates in the sacrifice of life itself in the dying process. The latter is not the end of the journey but the fullness of the transformative process. In this life the intensity of God's love is so great that "no one can see God and live." To live with this love in the human condition allows the unfolding of the knowledge of God to take place through our becoming one with Christ.

In traditional Christian thinking the imitation of Christ is the process by which we know God by becoming God, as far as that is possible, just as the Father knows the Son by becoming the Son. In the Trinity, the Father lives in the Son, not in himself, and the Son in the Father, not in himself. Christ gives himself totally to the Father and in doing so manifests who the Father is. As Jesus puts it, "Whoever has seen me has seen the Father" (John 14:9). In Christ's passion and self-emptying, we see what the Father is doing eternally in regard to the divine essence. He is divinity in the fullest sense by giving it away. The Trinity is infinite unity and infinite diversity at the same time.

The mind and heart of Christ are communicated to us through the Mystical Body of Christ, in which not only are we one with the Father, the Son, and the Holy Spirit, but we are also one with each other in whom the same Mystery is dwelling and unfolding.

Whenever something horrendous enters our lives, the question to ask is: "Is this the sacrifice of Isaac that God is asking of me?" The willingness to sacrifice everything is an essential part of our spiritual journey and enables us to be conformed to the cross of Christ. The suffering of Christ on the cross is God's supreme invitation to enter into the life of the Trinity.

# 6

## THE PROCESS OF CENTERING PRAYER

EVERYTHING IS ROOTED in the ultimate Oneness of the Trinity. Everything comes forth from there and returns there. It might be of interest to approach this divine mystery from the perspective of centering prayer itself. That would give us an opportunity to deepen our understanding of the progress of centering prayer as it unfolds into the advancing stages of contemplation and higher levels of consciousness. *Higher* isn't exactly the right word here. "Higher" suggests a judgment, whereas the highest level of consciousness is without judgment. It is neither high nor low, nor right or left. Everything is subsumed into the Oneness of the Ultimate Mystery. We all, in the measure of our limitations, are accessing this Mystery, which is *the* greatest reality, and in some sense the *only* reality. Everything else is filtered through our consciousness. This filtering normally involves the prejudices of our cultural conditioning and the biases of our emotional programs for happiness.

When we initiate centering prayer, we are entering into the consensual process of welcoming God into our inmost being and allowing him to love us according to his will. Our penetration of that presence is totally up to God. Some folks penetrate farther into it than others, but everybody enjoys it to the fullness of their capacity. Centering prayer is a direct route to the apophatic experience of contemplation in the Christian tradition.

Centering prayer, if you do it with some degree of correctness, gradually disestablishes the false self along with its symptoms. These symptoms are listed by Saint Paul: hatred, jealousy, violence, anger, ambition, division, envy (Galatians 5:20). The consequences of false self convictions and behavior due to the inevitable frustrations of the emotional programs for happiness are gradually brought to our attention by the Holy Spirit; not, of course, to dwell on or to act out, but rather to develop the habit of promptly letting go of them.

Letting go does not free us from the primitive energies that we inherit from our ancestors whether human, animal, or vegetative. It is a path to freedom and to the awakening of the true self, which is the image of God in us that Genesis reveals, and which is a participation in the divine light according to the Prologue to John's gospel. The text states that "the Word of God enlightens everyone coming into the world" (1:9). Everyone, in virtue of being human, is thus in relationship to the Eternal Word of God.

Paul's term for the Eternal Word is *Christ*, so when the Word enters into the human situation, the whole human family becomes the Body of God. This teaching is thoroughly developed in the Epistle to the Romans and in other parts of scripture.

When we take our position for centering prayer, we are not just parking ourselves on a bench or cushion or on the floor. We are sitting down in God. We are sitting down with our false self and with our true self. At first, our chief experience is the false self with its thunderous barrage of thoughts and tormenting desires. These prevent us from experiencing the more subtle levels of the true self.

By practicing centering prayer, we hope to manifest less of the symptoms of the false self and its frustrations, and experience the symptoms of the true self. These are summarized theologically as the Fruits and Gifts of the Spirit, which are: charity, joy, peace, patience, kindness, long-suffering, affability, goodness, fidelity, gentleness, and self-control. If you are experiencing a greater love for God that is not looking for reward this is the work of the Spirit in you. It is one of the Fruits of the Spirit and a participation in Christ consciousness.

In the inner room that we access through the method of centering prayer, there are various levels of the unconscious. One is the ontological, which includes the Fruits and Gifts of the Spirit and the theological infused virtues, all of which are designed to transform our behavior and attitudes into the mind and heart of Christ. The Fruits and Gifts of the Spirit are signs that this process is taking place. We don't "do" them; they "do" us in response to our growing freedom from the straitjacket of the false self, with its limiting, confining, confusing, and at times tormenting thoughts and desires. The false self is rooted in illusion, the mistaken idea of ourselves that arises largely from the pre-rational period of infancy and early childhood. Judgments about what is right and wrong are often imposed on us through the culture we live in or by our own ignorance. Neither represent reality as it is.

The divine omnipresence means that God is present everywhere and in everything that exists in virtue of the fact that nothing can exist if he is not present. Every creature depends on him and the ongoing evolution of creation. This is not a one-time process but something that is happening moment by moment. We must think of God as in constant movement. God in fact is total activity and total rest at the same time. He is in relationship to everything that exists, and hence knows all of reality through and through.

At the end of each day of the six days of creation, God is described as saying that his work was "good," and after creating the human species, he said that it was "very good." God delights in his creatures, even with all their many faults and limitations. From his eternal point of view, the ultimate transformation of humanity is present to him, along with all its very real limitations.

We are told that God on the first day of creation commands, "Let there be light," but this is not the sun or the moon or the stars. "Let there be light" is the transcendent creative light that is present as the basic energy of everything that exists (see Genesis 1:3). All other lights are secondary compared to this one. It is that light that is the source of the spiritual nature of our being. It is that light that dwells in us as our inmost spiritual nature, and that is the light that will judge us at the time of our passing from this earthly life. Our own inner light will be our judge and show us exactly who we are and the true state of our relationship with God.

In order to prepare for that moment and to cultivate the light, a practice of relating to God at the level that can access this spiritual light is an important aspect of religion. The essential job of religion is to facilitate and support us in the journey into the light, which is synonymous with the true self. The point of discussing it is to make ourselves aware of the height, length, breadth, and depth of the love of Christ in taking on our human nature.

The concerns, distractions, achievements, ambitions, and other human activities are often monumental, awesome, and frightening. And yet, compared to God's plan, they are nothing at all. The contemplative vision perceives God even in the midst of disaster, turmoil, or personal failure. It never loses hope because its hope is not based on human events but on the divine goodness, which is infinitely powerful and infinitely merciful. Theological hope makes even the greatest of sinners candidates for the highest beatitude. It takes God only a moment to transform someone, as in the case of the Good Thief (see Luke 23:39–43).

Centering prayer brings us into the movement of contemplation. We sit down to consent, and the first thing we do is forget about everything we were concerned about. When you have been practicing this for some years, you may feel attracted to extending it for half an hour, forty minutes, or even for an hour twice a day. Everybody is at a different place in their spiritual journey, but once in a while one might reflect on whether the amount of time that one is giving to centering prayer is proportionate to the amount of stress, anxiety, and work that one has to do. Balance between silence and activity is required. This does not necessarily mean total silence, because action also has an essential role to play in our transformation.

The interaction between periods of silence and activity that is appropriate for us in our state of life and the social duties in which we find ourselves, has to be taken into account. Time spent in waiting for God, or waiting upon God, or in doing nothing, is not lost time. It is cultivating the attitude of acceptance of our whole being. Our inmost being does not have to prove itself because it is already infinitely loved. At the deepest level it is free, joyful, full of love, compassion, and an awareness of the unity of all that exists. This includes the unity of the human family and fosters a sense of responsibility for it.

We are both individual and social at the same time. Right now, Western society has moved into a very individualistic frame of reference. As a result, there is a movement to recover community in various forms. People have always understood the value of community, but community from the Middle Ages up to the Enlightenment was overemphasized to the diminution of a proper proportion of respect for the individual. That led to the domination of social factors over individuals, whether political or ecclesial. God is not only calling every individual into direct union with himself, but also *into communion with everyone else* who is being called to the same thing, and to experience in some degree the fact that we belong to God and to one another. In some way, we may feel called, at times, to bear each others' burdens, and that includes the psychological damage that our false selves have done to us.

A human body contains cells that are no longer healthy. The healthy cells are meant to build up new cells to replace those that are diminishing in their effectiveness. Every cell in the body has a mission; it is not just a needless multiplication of simple forms of life. Each cell contains the whole program for growth of the particular organism that it serves.

The human soul fills every part of the body and gives it its direction and form. The Holy Spirit as the soul of the Mystical Body fills each one of its cells with the divine DNA, so each cell has the whole program of what the

Mystical Body is supposed to be. Paul speaks of the mature age of Christ, which he calls the *pleroma,* when Christ will be everything in everyone (see Colossians 2:9).

The first step of centering prayer is the intention to sit down with the willingness to be transformed into the divine image within. Christ is the Son of God made human and the divine-human way of being in the world. We don't achieve that by leaving society or jumping off a bridge, but by submitting to the movement of both the good and the evil that exists in each of us. Not that we subscribe to the evil. Jesus simply taught, "Do not resist an evildoer" (Matthew 5:39). What does that mean?

At the very least, we accept what is and stay open to what the Spirit might ask us to do. It is not sheer passivity, but a detachment from action that is merely a reaction to circumstances or evils done to us. We are thus enabled to take steps to correct situations as they emerge. Discernment grows along with contemplative prayer. As one's perspective of reality is purified of the influences of the false self, both social and psychological, it begins to perceive the way things really are and is sensitive to the movements of the Spirit within our inmost being. The spontaneous manifestation of the risen life of Christ in us through the Fruits and Gifts of the Spirit and the theological virtues flows out of this source. One surrenders to them, submits to them, or collaborates with them as they arise in daily life. They are extremely practical because they extend to the smallest details of daily life. Thus, God is interested in absolutely everything we do, and every action is recorded. Reality never forgets.

Everything that happens is forever insofar as it is real. It is only the false self that dies. That is a happy death in God because it is a movement into true freedom and the fullness of life. As we let go of our concerns, centering prayer becomes an exercise of just being. *Resting in God* is the classical term given for it. Resting may suggest doing nothing. However, it is not *actually* doing nothing; it is letting go of our thoughts and desires in order to allow the divine action to work freely in us.

Opening to the Spirit by way of intention ushers us into the inner room that Jesus refers to in his wisdom saying in Matthew 6:6. The application of the practical consequences of just being is the termination of our endless interior dialogue. As we enter the inner room in centering prayer, having established silence about what is going on outside of us and the environment that we are in, we let go of all mental activity. Put a note at the entrance of your inner room that says, "Drop the interior dialogue," or, "Leave your false self here." We might add, "Don't pick it up again when you leave."

The false self is manifested by a constant stream of thoughts that are inappropriate, unwanted, crazy, or horrible. These can be memories, plans, and desires, and here the principle of resisting no evil is very important. You don't resist the fact of having unwanted thoughts and still less do you fight them. In addition, don't fuss over the fact that you are still experiencing so many distractions after so many years of centering prayer practice.

The capacity to ruminate, think, or daydream is endless. The imagination is a perpetual-motion faculty, so that what we are actually doing is reducing the energy we put into pursuing false self reflections, desires, and experiences that may arise during the time of prayer.

What centering prayer offers is a method for the first two steps of Jesus's recommendation in Matthew 6:6 to enter our inner room and close the door. It seems to me that prayer in secret is so silent that it really belongs to the realm of infused contemplation. Perhaps it is the word or phrase that Jesus used for what later became known in the Christian tradition as contemplative prayer in the strict sense of the word.

We cannot enter the contemplative state on our own. We can only reduce the obstacles to it, and that is what the first two steps are: exterior silence and interior silence. We are then on the edge of nowhere, which is everywhere. The sound of silence is the habit of listening and the training of our spiritual will to abide in this simple turning to God. That can be done through various symbols, such as returning to the sacred word, a sacred glance, or briefly noticing our breath. These are simply expressions of the spiritual intent that maintains our consent, or at least our will to consent, to the presence and action of the Spirit within us.

Consenting to God's action in daily life is consenting to

what happens. In our commitment in baptism, we join Jesus in his baptism, or rather he joins us in ours. We descend into the baptismal waters, the symbol of tribulation where the false self dies, and we rise out of the waters of tribulation through faith in his resurrection. The Spirit of Christ becomes the primary motive for all our activities.

An insight that is significant is that every aspect of our life is included in our basic perception of God, of the Church, and of the spiritual life. In a previous chapter I spoke of Joseph giving up his two eyes and becoming blind to his original vision of life with Mary and Jesus. His life with Mary was scrambled by her mysterious pregnancy. Later, the disappearance of Jesus in the Temple without telling his parents was a call for Joseph to give up his role as his father according to Jewish custom. He had formally accepted that responsibility, and it ended when Jesus said that his father was somebody else.

If that is a correct interpretation, it may signify that in order to realize and become one's vision, you have to give it up—or at least be willing to let God do something else with it. God often reaffirms the vision, as we saw, once that willingness to let go is present. In other words, *detachment* from our vision is an important factor in reaching it. It is not our idea of it that achieves it. Rather our idea hinders it. The freedom to accept reality as it is and as it happens seems to be the primary transforming experience of the spiritual journey.

At some point after establishing a daily practice of centering prayer and moving into deeper silence, it becomes habitual, so that you may be able to enter immediately into a place of relative silence and peace. There, Jesus recommends praying in secret because, "Your Father who sees in secret will reward you." The word *reward* has a meaning that is much more expansive than we normally think. It is much more than repayment for a job well done.

In a couple of verses prior, the same word appears when Jesus refers to certain Pharisees who prayed on street corners with a view to being seen by the public and applauded for their good works. In that passage, the word *reward* is clearly limited to "they have received their reward." *Reward* in Matthew 6:6 is a different Hebrew word, and it implies in its Aramaic roots the full blossoming of human nature: the releasing of all the supernatural powers that are present within us and their coming to full bloom, and flourishing. Thus, the text refers to three or four symbols of the transformative process and reinforces the promise of transformation, to which the Gospel is continually inviting us.

Through prayer in secret we begin to forget ourselves. Over time, our willingness to accept the prayer just as it is becomes more and more based on pure faith. This means that God is present whether we feel him as absent or present. That insight frees us from needless anxiety and wrong-headed expectations. God vastly surpasses any experience of God that we can have, and that is perhaps why Jesus uses the word "secret."

The silence of the false self may still include thoughts, but one is aware that one is not interested in them and not seeking them. Sometimes the attraction to silence is deep enough that one has no thoughts at all for a certain period of time. This is the beginning of the awakening of the true self. Consciousness without particular content is contemplative prayer. Consciousness that is not self-conscious is an even more advanced experience that may take place as prayer in secret stabilizes.

Jesus points to it only in general, because it may have many forms, but it always includes the Fruits of the Spirit. These Fruits lead to an increase in selfless love, the sense of well-being and joy, the recognition that the experience is impossible to explain, and that everything is perfect just as it is. The latter is an insight the Zen Buddhists also attest to when they speak of enlightenment. Enlightenment does not mean one is not fully aware that something has to be done to correct the injustices and violence in the world, but there is no emotional anxiety, and it does not cause suffering. It is compassion without suffering.

The sense of well-being and joy also expresses itself as empathy that is able to see every situation in its full extent, including the need to do something about some very real problem, but without the compulsion to do it oneself, unless one feels called by God to resolve it. One is aware of the distress and is in sympathy with it. One is willing to bear its burdens by inwardly accepting what sufferings might come our way for the redemption of the human family: in other words, allowing the divine energies to flow through us to the rest of the Mystical Body somewhat the way the healing bodily energies function in the human body.

Once interior silence during prayer is well established, time passes in a flash, and contemplative prayer in the strict sense mentioned earlier has taken place. The spontaneous exercise of the Fruits and Gifts of the Spirit and the Beatitudes in daily life also manifests the awakening of the true self. Periods of unloading and purification of the unconscious may also continue. These can be redeeming not just for ourselves, but for others. In other words, as we get well, everybody else in the Mystical Body is going to get better, too. In other words, if we can stop pouring the negative energies of our false self into the universe, the universe is going to improve.

In fact, it improves without our thinking about it. This does not exclude planning and the use of technology to improve negative situations, but there is not the anxiety that sometimes characterizes well intentioned people who want to fix everything and have not found out yet that they cannot even fix themselves. To be a channel or an instrument of divine love is the greatest contribution we can make to humanity. This is why those who work for Contemplative Outreach are doing most when they are faithful to their daily practice, which is opening and preparing them to become channels of God's love.

Let us summarize what we are trying to do in the practice of centering prayer. Letting go of our external circumstances symbolized by choosing a solitary spot and introducing the sacred symbol of our intention constitute the dispositions that we are cultivating, which might be called *acceptance*. Acceptance, however, can be hesitant at times, as when it is time for prayer and we are immersed in other things and feel reluctant to sit down. In this case, be sure to sit down anyway.

Thus, acceptance is not yet *consent*, which welcomes the formal time of prayer no matter how reluctant we may feel. Prayer for us has become a necessity. It also carries a sense of coming home, experiencing one's inmost being, or even of resting in our heavenly Father's lap. Consent has the added element of wanting to do God's will and of disregarding any factors that might hinder that commitment.

That would coincide with interior silence, or the second step, which is "closing the door," meaning closing the door on our interior dialogue. Remember, the password to the inner room is *Stop the interior dialogue*.

Whatever is bothering you, whatever you are thinking about, whatever memories are rising up, whatever your plans are—this is not the time to think of them. Similarly, one encounters no resistance to the imposition or intrusion of thoughts that are inappropriate or unwanted. One simply lets them come and lets them go. Some people find the image of boats floating on the surface of a river helpful, or being at the bottom of a river and looking up and seeing them all go by. In any case, *let them all go by*.

Our intention is not always something we are fully aware of, but it can be cultivated through centering prayer, so that sometimes you are aware that you are not interested in any thoughts and that your attention, however general, is integrated and focused. Still, particular thoughts go by, but they recede from your *attention* and are easily disregarded, like background music at the supermarket, which you can't help being aware of but pay no attention to.

Prayer in secret might be called *stillness*. This is the third step. It corresponds to the recommendation of the Psalms: "Be still, and know that I am God" (Psalm 46:10). This is the place of surrender and the complete gift of ourselves to God. We are beginning to find out who we really are. The true self is manifesting through the experience of the Fruits and Gifts of the Spirit that may emerge on those first two levels, but which manifest themselves more clearly and frequently when the sense of stillness is present.

Stillness can have different degrees during formal prayer. One consists of periods of consciousness without mental content. Time is the measure of motion; that is the classical definition. So when your eyes are turned inwardly toward the deep self, only thoughts are moving. When there are no thoughts, there is no movement and hence no sense of time. This state is a kind of preview of what eternity is, which is not a long time, but no time at all.

It comes as a surprise when the bell to end the prayer period rings because when you sat down, that was the last thought you had. Would that we could always be in that space! It is extremely refreshing. One comes out of that space feeling energized, loved, and at peace; or that everything is okay; or that even the worst of problems is secondary to the pervasive, all-embracing presence that has no name or form, and that is just *presence*. Contemplation may unfold beyond that experience into what might be called *pure consciousness*, which is an intensification of consciousness without content.

This state of sheer receptivity is welcoming and enables the Spirit to manifest the truth more frequently in our lives. The true self begins to be a reality for us. Meanwhile, because of the vulnerability that this prayer provides, we welcome the unloading of the unconscious if traumatic experiences, warehoused in the body from early childhood, that need to be evacuated. Our defenses dissolve in this process, so nothing prevents the body with its marvelous capacity for health to evacuate the emotional sludge of earlier times. It does this through the flow of unwanted thoughts. Emotional junk is a block to the circulation of bodily and spiritual energies. Awareness of the movements of grace that activate the Fruits and the Gifts of the Spirit is also blocked by undigested emotional debris.

The Gifts of the Spirit, which are aspects of the true self, are worth looking at from time to time, not so much to see if we are practicing them, but just to be aware of the extent of the empowerment that God has given us. In a sense, *we are overqualified for the transformative process*. Most people think that because they feel themselves to be unworthy, they are not invited. Divine wisdom, however, reveals that it is precisely our weakness that interests God, more than anything else (see 2 Corinthians 12:7).

His desire to heal us is in direct proportion to our confidence that in spite of all the obstacles in our lives and our personal defects, God is sympathetic to our basic goodwill and the union with him that our hearts are longing for. We become aware of an ever deeper longing to be united with God, to be embraced by God, or to put it even more strongly, to be kissed and engulfed by the divine embrace, as we read in the Song of Songs, "Let him kiss me with the kisses of his mouth" (Song of Songs 1:2). The mystics have understood God's mouth to be the Holy Spirit and our mouth to be our spiritual will. When this intention is thoroughly established, the will has a continuous open mouth, so to speak, to receive whatever nourishment God, like a mother bird, wants to put into it.

To be all mouth in this sense is to be totally willing to be penetrated and transformed by the Spirit of God in whatever way is possible for us and that includes the willingness to be purified of the unconscious junk of a lifetime. When moments of unloading occur, they may be so strong as to make it impossible to access the usual silence and peace during formal prayer. There may be periods when we just have to put up with the barrage of thoughts and feelings, including primitive emotions that come from early life memories or cultural influences.

Christ consciousness, which is the full exercise of the ontological unconscious, has now become active with its various capacities through the theological virtues of faith, hope, and charity, and the Fruits and Gifts of the Spirit. These dispositions unite us with God and with other people, nature, and the universe. They awaken the sense of belonging to the universe and the need of stewardship for the animal, plant, and mineral kingdoms. One enters into the command of Yahweh in Genesis to subdue irrational nature (1:28). This does not mean to dominate. *Subdue* is a Hebrew word that means to get underneath and to support something from below. The image comes from shepherding. So humans should be good shepherds of the universe in all its aspects and care for animals and the rest of the natural world as loving caregivers.

This consciousness awakens the true self, with its freedom from us and the domination of our emotions. This consciousness does not do away with our emotions, but enables them to be deeply felt without putting us into a mood and causing negative reactions. Instead, the emotions become the appropriate responses to each situation as it arises.

Actually, this consciousness gives one the capacity to be more involved with the world and with everybody's problems as they come into our lives, without being overly upset or unduly concerned by anything. One's consciousness is rooted in the mysterious perfection of everything just as it is. Such is God's perception of reality because he knows all its inner workings and its final marvelous resolution.

The emergence of this consciousness leads to the final stage, which might be called, and I borrow the term from David Frenette, *incarnational contemplation*. This means that we incarnate the contemplative state or the true self into our lives and activities. It implies the full exercise of the Fruits and Gifts of the Spirit as they manifest in us.

This stage takes away the uneasiness we may feel between how much silence and how much activity we are called to. The Spirit guides us because we are never really separated from God. We have penetrated the veil of the senses to the point that although God is not apparent, he is accepted and loved in every creature and in everything that happens, including suffering, pain, and disappointment.

With the establishing of this state of mind, God can no longer hide behind secondary causes. The infusion of divine love tends to increase. Our preoccupations shield us from the intensity of divine love. As they diminish, this intensity increases. Then everything is done out of love, and everything is the reception of divine love.

The movement of centering prayer is toward the integration of silence and activity, activity not based on a naive confidence in ourselves, but rather as a response to the presence and action of the Spirit that is more and more the guiding light in all our activities.◆

# PART III

CONSENTING
TO
TRANSFORMATION
ACCORDING
TO GOD'S TERMS

*In 2009 we explored together the higher levels of consciousness and I stressed the importance of not attaching ourselves to any attempt to reach them. Transformation must be sought on God's terms and we are simply called to consent to the process. The last talk offered in 2009 was on the archetypes of human development. Much has been written on this subject, and mine are simply some off-the-cuff remarks suggesting an additional model of the transformative process to those described in the Spiritual Journey tapes to help grasp their common elements.*

# 7

# THE CROSS OF CHRIST

IN THE BUDDHIST–CHRISTIAN dialogue there is an intriguing juxtaposition of symbols. A favorite one is Buddha sitting in the lotus position. This posture expresses an attitude of complete repose and equanimity. The delicate smile on his lips arises from his having risen above all suffering. It is a primary symbol of human self-realization and enlightenment.

This posture of the Buddha expresses his teaching about human integration, liberation from suffering, and the attainment of that sublime equanimity that the Buddhists say is already present in everyone. We simply don't believe it. That denial keeps forcing itself upon us and is our chief problem. It convinces us to think we are separate from God.

In this striking symbol of the Buddha there is a sense of complete attainment of all that human beings are intended to be and already are. It was in seeing a reclining statue of the Buddha that Thomas Merton received an awakening of his own, which he recounts in his *Asian Journal*.

Let us compare the tranquil face of the Buddha with the face of Christ on the cross. According to Christian faith, Jesus Christ not only attained full enlightenment, but actually *is* one with the divine nature and is possessed by it.

Christ's face is very different from the peaceful smile of the Buddha. His lips are distorted in pain. His face is that of a person undergoing unbearable torture and inward agony. He is abandoned by all human support, physically and spiritually rejected by the civil and religious authorities of his time, and by his own disciples who fled from the scene.

Christ on the cross seems to be the opposite of spiritual attainment, and yet this reality is put before us as the very center of the Christian religion.

These images represent the essence of two of the most sophisticated world religions, and they seem to be irreconcilable. Both are believed to be symbols of Ultimate Reality, and in a very real sense not only symbols, but the Reality itself. If we can hold these two apparent opposites in dynamic tension, how does Jesus manifest in his suffering and absolute privation the same Ultimate Reality that the Buddha manifests with his smile of supreme serenity and absolute fulfillment?

If Christ on the cross is the greatest manifestation of who God is as taught by the Christian religion, then who is this God who does not come to the aid of his Son, whom he loves beyond all things? There is no answer in rational consciousness to the dilemma of transcending suffering and at the same time being fully immersed in it. The paradox reveals that from the perspective of the highest consciousness death and resurrection are revealing one and the same reality. In confronting this paradox one gets an intuition into the fact that God cannot be fully manifested either by death or resurrection, but only by both at once.

"If you want to save your life," (meaning your false self or ego) "you will bring yourself to ruin. But if you bring yourself to nothing for my sake you will find out who you are" (Matthew 10:39).*

Who we are then is not anybody we think we are. We are not our résumé. Who we are is not the ego that we try to get to know if we are thinking of making friends or marrying somebody and we want to know what makes them tick. Who we are is not even the true self, which is the image of God in us.

Who you think you are depends on the emphasis you give to each of these words. *Who* are you? is your résumé. Who *are* you? is your ego, the personality that you present to the world. Who are *you*? is the true self, but still not ultimately who you are. Theologians have not settled this

---

* *New American Bible, The Vatican II Weekday Missal for Monday of the 15th Week in Ordinary Time.* Copyright by the Confraternity of Christian Doctrine, 1970.

question. The mystics have had some ideas about it. In any case, who are *you*? is whom Jesus is talking to.

"You will find out," Jesus says, "if you bring yourself to no-thing," to a non-possessive attitude toward everything including yourself, life or death, future or past, or any category of the human time–space continuum.

This is the experience that Jesus is interested in transmitting to us because it is the very life of the Father.

The eternal Son of God has become human. This is the meaning of the Incarnation. The primary mission of the Son is to reveal the Father. That is why contemporary theologians are backing off from the idea that we were redeemed in the sense of being paid for like slaves.

Redemption is something much more profound. It is the total healing of human nature with all its wounds as a result of wrong choices throughout the course of our own life and humanity's evolution. It is the return to who we really are and the freedom to manifest God in every detail of life.

What God seems to be doing is to put the extraordinary capacity of human beings for divine union into the worst possible situation to see what happens. This movement makes sense once we grasp what God is doing all the time, which is giving himself away in love.

The Trinitarian mystery is the explanation for all reality, which begins with the eternal persons of the Trinity. The Father begets the Son for all eternity. The infinite possibilities contained in the Father come to actuality in the Son. The

Father expresses all that he is in the Son. That is an essential insight into the meaning of suffering. In the Trinity, sacrifice—which is another word for self-surrender and giving oneself away in perfect love—is delightful. Beatitude takes place when there are no obstacles of a self to get in the way.

God's delight is to give all that he is to the Son. The Father and the Son breathe forth a third Person, the Holy Spirit of God, who is the quintessence of their mutual self-giving love. They live in each other rather than in themselves, forever giving themselves away.

Suppose, however, that the Son, who is actualizing all the potentialities of the Father, is sent by the Father to enter creation and to become a participant in the human situation in which one of its capacities is freedom of choice.

The revelation of Christ is that "God so loved the world that he sent his Son" to manifest the divine nature in the lowest form of intelligence we know of in this universe (see John 3:16). As Saint Paul puts it in Philippians 2:6, the Word of God did not consider being *equal* to God something to hang on to. One can hardly push a non-possessive attitude beyond that. In other words, he who is everything and who has everything wants to give it all away. This is the most extraordinary revelation of who God is: non-possessive love. In Greek this is called *agape* or pure love, a love that seeks no reward and has no attachment to itself.

Christ was sent by the Father from the world of pure love and non-possessiveness into a world of evolving creatures with all the animal instincts that we still possess in our bodies and brains.

The scientist and paleontologist Pierre Teilhard de Chardin taught that biological evolution was now coming to an end. He believed that the evolution of humanity is shifting its focus from the biological development of the human body and brain to the *spiritual evolution of consciousness*. That is, consciousness can unite the fractured relationships of the human family by revealing their rootedness, oneness, and common destiny in an intelligence that is higher than rational consciousness and penetrated by the love of the Holy Spirit. The Spirit is trying to manifest in a species that is virtually the opposite of God from almost every perspective. This reminds us of the adventurousness of God. He is interested in transforming the most unlikely characters. At least, he clearly states in the Gospel that "the Son of Man has come to seek that which was lost" (Luke 19:10)—that is, those who are totally wiped out and utterly abandoned.

The Son of God, according to the Gospel, gave up infinite happiness, power, and majesty in order to identify with human nature subject to the evolutionary process of material creation. The very words that John uses in the prologue to his gospel—"The Word became flesh"—is not primarily about physical bodies. It is about human nature perceived as fallen, or which we might think of today as *unevolved*.

Perhaps both are true, just like the smile of the Buddha and the tortured lips of Jesus are the same reality manifested in two different expressions.

The Word made flesh is the dispossession of the glory, majesty, and dignity that Christ deserved as the Son of the Father in order to become a slave, as Paul said (see Philippians 2:7). Thus, Jesus identified himself with us on every level of human misery, including living and dying in a world filled with the consequences of sin itself.

Regarding Christ's passion, Paul makes the statement that Jesus, the Christ, was made *sin* for our sake (2 Corinthians 5:21). The price of that acceptance is revealed in the Passion narratives, especially in Christ's agony in the Garden of Gethsemane, where he pleaded with the Father not to have to go through this identification with sin (see Matthew 26:36–46). The baptism of John the Baptist was a baptism of repentance. Why would Christ seek to be baptized by John if he had no sin? Jesus descended into the water of the Jordan because he wanted to manifest his identification with the human condition of weakness and sinfulness.

He enters into the waters for our sake, and then, driven by the Spirit, retired into the desert to experience the raw nature of human temptation and sin.

What is this human nature that Jesus took to himself? "All flesh shall see the salvation of God," we read in Luke 3:6 and Isaiah 40:5. What is this "flesh"? It is a term that refers to the human condition precisely as fallen. In the scripture, the concept of "fallen" appears in the story of Adam and Eve, in which they forfeited their intimate union with God when they ate the forbidden fruit of the Tree of the Knowledge of Good and Evil.

When that disposition confronts the fact of one species of animal evolving into rational consciousness, there is a problem. All creatures can only be imperfect. Only God is perfect. Perhaps God chose the lowest form of intelligent species that we know of to be incarnate because he wanted to let go of his glory to the furthest possible extent. In other words, God does not seem to care about being God.

Since God cannot die and experience the nothingness of creatures, he wanted to become one of us so he could experience firsthand what it is like to identify with the human predicament and to experience death.

In the story of Adam and Eve, God made them sharers in the divine nature from the beginning of their existence. Scripture says that he visited them every day in the cool of the evening. Evidently, they had a wonderful relationship with God. But he warned them, "Do not eat of the Tree of the Knowledge of Good and Evil, for then you will die" (see Genesis 2:17). The Tree of the Knowledge of Good and Evil is the symbol of self-consciousness. Eating its fruit brought a sense of being separated from God.

The demon's temptation was a masterstroke. It is the greatest of all temptations: "No, you're not going to die if you eat of the tree. You will be equal to God, knowing good and evil" (see 3:4–5). Thus, the great temptation into which Adam and Eve fell was to become God *on their own terms*.

I suspect that this is a temptation that almost every human being experiences at some point. Our destiny, as established by God, is to become God, too. We may not be open to that idea at first because we think it might mean the loss of our self-identity and all the efforts we put into building up the idea of ourselves that we call ego.

Adam and Eve were not sinning in wanting to be God, because that was God's will for them and for all humanity. Their mistake was that they wanted to be God *on their own terms*. God wanted them to become God *on his terms*: that is, to let go of their separate-self sense and the false self that it creates.

As human beings, we find ourselves at the peak of an evolutionary process that has culminated in a new way of relating to reality, which is self-consciousness. This does not emerge until about six or eight months into a baby's life. Then, it is subject to the emotional programs of happiness that it invented to endure the cultural climate it is being brought up in. It develops a false self based on its demands for the gratification of its felt need for survival and security, power and control, and affection and esteem, rather than in the experience of spiritual and Divine Reality.

Science is now discovering that the brain is developing in a way that our ancestors could not have experienced.

There is no evidence that the evolution of our brain is going to stop. If we survive as a species, there seems to be an evolutionary movement or élan that is moving us toward the ultimate purpose God had in creation, which is to share the divine life with us, not only individually but corporately as the human family.

What would further evolution look like? The teachers of the world religions have described their experience of it, and the Buddha and Jesus Christ have manifested it, each in their own respective lifetimes. But what it means for us right now is that we are in a transition period between animal consciousness and awakened human beings.

Religion is designed to guide and introduce us into this fully human consciousness and into what lies beyond it, which is the development of rational consciousness into the divine consciousness.

The discipline of centering prayer teaches us how to consent to this transforming process. The first thing we have to accept is the human condition, which is our personal experience of the weakness of our human nature. The proper response is not shame or guilt, but acceptance of our limitations, knowing that this is what attracts the divine mercy.

Since God cannot cease to be God, his next best choice in sharing the infinite goodness with us seems to be to make us partakers in the divine nature, insofar as this is possible. Sharing the divine life with every creature according to its capacity is God's way of being not-God, a manifestation of his infinite humility.

The cross of Christ is the symbol of the human condition. Crucified between heaven and earth, we humans cannot ascend on our own power into divine transformation, and we cannot regress to the irresponsibility that is the condition of our animal nature. We cannot find fulfillment in the pleasures of the natural world, and we cannot move beyond our incomplete human condition into the wisdom that human consciousness is meant to become through the evolutionary process.

Some are becoming human, but most have not reached it yet. Beyond being fully human is the possibility of becoming divinely human after the example of Jesus Christ. In view of all this, we are in a transition period of human history that could scarcely be more painful. God's project is to identify with "fallen" or "unevolved" human nature, depending on which explanation you may choose. The bottom line is the same. We cannot do it ourselves.

Looking at the crucifix, our first act is the acceptance of where we are, which is to be part of the present transitional period, which may be the most difficult one in the whole evolutionary process.

The cross without a body on it is the symbol of the human condition as we are experiencing it now. If you look closely, it is the negation of our "I."

That is the project we are invited by God to accept,

along with all the conditions that are the result of the evolutionary process. The practical conclusion is that our weakness, guilt, shame, disappointment, or failure are part of the human condition. To accept them is to be willing to enter into the meaning of the Cross. The process of no-selfing, so to speak, is at the same time the process of uniting with God.

## 8

## Notes on Divine Union, Unity, and Beyond

W E HAVE BEEN discussing the full development of the spiritual journey and divine union and unity. This is not only a difficult subject, but it is one that is almost impossible to articulate. It is worth mentioning that the vocabulary, at least in English, is somewhat dominated by Eastern terminology and experience. For example, the discussion of unity consciousness and non-duality does not appear as a term in most of the mystical literature of the West.

What is called the stage of unity consciousness is the permanent experience of oneness with God. It is a state of consciousness that is beyond reflection. In other words, it is the disappearance of the separate self-sense. As a result, one is always living with and in God. It is not just union with God, which is still a conscious relationship of two, however much they are surrendered to each other. The greatest experience of God is no experience because we do not have the faculties that can perceive this level. Unity consciousness is not dependent on any signs or symbols of God, nor on rituals or liturgies, because in a sense it has made us one with God; it does not have any further needs. Is there any experience of self at all at this level of divine unity?

Perhaps the German mystic Meister Eckhart and the Beguines of Northern Europe in the thirteenth century are the most explicit on this subject in the Christian tradition. Saint John of the Cross seems to hint at it, but even he is not too specific. Saint Teresa of Ávila does not touch on these things, at least not in the language that we are using today. Such words as *non-dual, nirvana, enlightenment, Advaitic Hinduism,* or *Vedanta* are all becoming familiar terms in the West to those on the spiritual journey.

We need to be aware of them if we are going to guide others on the spiritual journey. We spoke about the non-dual and have heard descriptions of it such as "not one, not two"; "not this, not that." These are descriptions that arose in the Asian spiritual traditions. It is hard for Christians to believe that people could acquire such high attainment unless they had first interiorized an enormous amount of grace.

To think of non-monotheists as pagans or even semi-demoniac is not only insulting, but childish. It does not recognize the extraordinary spiritual attainments of our brothers and sisters in the Buddhist, Hindu, Jain, Shinto, and Daoist religions who now challenge us as to whether there is anything comparable in the accepted spiritual teaching of the West. I am especially interested in inter-spiritual conversation, which is a further development of inter-religious dialogue, and which discusses the ultimate experience of the spiritual journey and transformative consciousness.

People who are approaching those areas of spiritual evolution are having an impact on society, because the energy they are channeling is so sublime that it secretly influences positive social events or decisions anywhere in the world.

A hazard involved in discussing these higher reaches of the spiritual journey is the fact that we do not know how to desire them without having had some experience of them. If we deliberately try to attain those states or stages, we are on the wrong road, because they come as the pure gift of God and spiritual evolution.

Some have come to an awakening experience with very little practical or mental preparation. Others have had a significant experience of God in childhood that they could not possibly have prepared themselves for. What centering prayer offers is a plan and practices *to reduce the obstacles to God's transforming action within*. In actual fact, there is a reservoir of ordinary people who have developed a base in conceptual understanding, practice, *and* ritual that has disposed them—body, soul, and mind—to become responsive to grace. As Jesus puts it, "Let anyone with ears, listen!" (Matthew 11:15).

Contemplative prayer builds on that foundation. Some New Age groups are naive in seeking to achieve on their own resources, through various self-help programs, the higher reaches of transformed consciousness that in fact are the pure gift of God.

I feel confident that in presenting the contemplative path to everyone who shows a sincere interest, we are responding to the image and likeness of God in them. Everybody has the potential to become not only contemplative, but to complete all the stages of contemplative development. From the perspective of God's infinite mercy, no one is worthy, but everyone is eligible and invited.

If we do not reach transformation by the end of our lives, there remains the dying process to complete it, or other programs that God may have established. In his teaching, Saint John of the Cross says that the night of spirit *is* purgatory, and that if you have been through that experience, nothing further by way of purification is required. Basically, the night of spirit frees us from the domination of our emotions, so that we can be completely liberated from the emotional programs for happiness formed by us in early childhood.

We are also freed from our false ideas of God that may hinder our relationship with him. These usually come from our culture and intellectual training, including our particular roles or anything that we were overidentified with. That includes our thoughts, personality, talents, professional skills, ministry, and even our religion. Everything that represents a possessive attitude is released or taken away in the night of spirit through the deep purification of the unconscious.

The night of spirit is the greatest gift God can impart apart from the beatific vision itself. If you do not pass through that cleansing at sufficient depth, you will have to have your wings dusted off after death in some purgatorial situation. Again, I want to emphasize that we do not get there under our own power or by any effort of ours. It depends entirely on God's will and his eternal plan for each of us.

You might reply, "Is this fair? Why doesn't God treat everybody the same?" He does treat everybody the same! There is no respect of persons in God. It is just that for some people, it is not yet time for the grace of divine union. Or they have not had adequate preparation, not only spiritually, but physiologically. The spiritual energies that are released in contemplative practice require a certain discipline of the body and nervous system to enable one to endure and handle the immense power of transforming energies.

The German theologian Karl Rahner taught that nature itself is graced. From that perspective, anybody just by being born has the capacity to open to the whole range of contemplative experience, whether it is completed in this life or by seeing God face to face in the beatific vision. The bottom line is that God is going to succeed in his redemptive plans, but on God's own terms.

Life lives itself with or without us. The unfolding experiences of everyday life and indeed of each moment is a continuing relationship and exchange with God. The divine adjusts itself to every creature with its level of consciousness just where it is.

God's creative power sustains every form of creation beginning with matter itself and the mineral world, then the plant and animal world, higher mammals, and finally us. God is never at a loss to bring about his intentions. Even events that may seem to us to be disasters have positive influences or effects that are hidden from us.

Take, for example, the horrendous Holocaust and genocides of various kinds that have multiplied in the last century, and that are still going on in parts of the world. How could anything good come out of them? To heal that situation is precisely the work that God has entrusted to us as co-creators of society. That is what human freedom is for.

The choice of surrender to God in whatever circumstances we are in is a transforming event. As we advance in the spiritual journey, we cannot claim as a right the transcendent states of divine union and unity. It depends on God's view of what is good for us and what our particular vocation is.

It is important not to have a self-centered or ambitious attitude toward higher stages of consciousness. Suppose, for example, that everybody goes into heaven ahead of you and you are the last person in the waiting line. It does not make any difference. What matters is the will of God. As one brilliant and mystical rabbi said in a lecture regarding transformation: "[It is] to *be* there without *getting* there."

Whatever we want to *get* is almost certainly a false-self project. *Receptivity* is greater than action because to *be* is greater than to *do*. It is not complete, however, until you can be contemplative along with any amount of action. God is always at rest, yet always supporting trillions of situations and projects of all kinds. We become like him by uniting contemplation and action as our spiritual evolution unfolds.

To be present to the present moment, to the work that we are doing, to the people we are talking to, or whatever ministry we may be engaged in, is a sign that grace is working in us. It is up to God to put us in divine union and, still more, in the state of unity consciousness. As mentioned above, if you think you can *get* it by your own efforts, however generous, this is a mistake. That is why, in presenting teaching about higher levels of consciousness to people who are beginners in the spiritual journey, we run the risk that they will start rolling up their sleeves in true North American fashion and try to work their way into it on their own.

The Pelagians were a group of early Christians who thought they could accomplish the higher reaches of the spiritual journey on their own. The Jansenists repeated the same mistake centuries later. To emphasize the divine plan once again: God wants to bring us into the most profound participation in the divine nature that is possible for humans, but *on his own terms*. Our own terms are false-self projects and will not work. It is not a personality or a self-aggrandizement issue. To emphasize this fact, let us say that God could not care less about worship and our good deeds. He already has all those things. There is nothing we can give him, in actual fact. It is for our sake that he calls us to worship and thanksgiving, because we have a profound need to praise and thank him.

The only thing that we can give him that no one else can is *to allow him to love us*. That may sound easy, but it is the hardest work of all of life's labors. To allow God to love us and to be, as individuals and as a race, the object of infinite love is an awesome responsibility. In a sense, it is doing nothing and everything at the same time. Out of the total surrender of ourselves comes the relatively effortless effectiveness of our service. At a certain point in our spiritual journey, the less we do the more God does.

What you do in the transformative process is not really your work. You realize instead that it is the divine energy operating within you as an instrument or as a channel, and that is what is effective. Our capacity to receive that energy and to share it is much more powerful than any merely personal initiative. In the beginning we have to make a lot of effort for spiritual growth just to find out that human effort does not work.

The wisdom of the Twelve Steps of AA has captured the essence of the Christian spiritual journey better than any other expression in modern times. It starts out in Step 1 with the conviction that "my life has become unmanageable"— so unmanageable, in fact, that in the case of alcoholics, it will lead to death unless they commit themselves to the remedy of AA practice. Every kind of addiction is paralyzing and needs the help of a community to support the healing process.

It is precisely the degree in which we recognize that we cannot do it ourselves that we perceive how desperately we need God to do it for us and in us. Turning ourselves over to God then becomes effective. For Christians on the spiritual journey, the night of sense introduces us to this rhythm. We do not bring about our improvement no matter how hard we try. The proper response becomes obvious: to turn our lives over completely to God's mercy.

The sixth and seventh steps are crucial in the program of AA. In the fifth step you make an inventory of all your faults in full detail and reveal them to the sponsor you have chosen and who has experience on the path of AA.

You would think the next step would be, "For God's sake, do something about this. Stop committing all these faults that are killing you!" But that is not the sixth step. The sixth step is to become *willing for God to take away our faults.* We are thus thoroughly convinced that we cannot do it ourselves. Our primary practice at this step is to become willing for God to take them away. We are not ready to pray for God to take them away until we are really *willing*, and that is what is causing the delay. We have deep, unconscious attachments to our faults, and in fact we rather like them.

The next step is to pray that God *will* actually take them away. To become willing to be healed is the main thrust of this sixth step. Saint Augustine in his early days of conversion confessed to God, "I desire to become chaste, but not just yet." That is a good example of the situation. In any case, to get there is not by trying. The only way to get there is to *be* there. And you can only *be put there* by the ever-forgiving and loving action of God.

In his well-known article "Emotional Sobriety," written in his mature years, Bill W. stated that he had learned that he did not attain sobriety by simply avoiding alcohol. He could only get it by going deeper into the *source* of his alcoholic problem and reaching *emotional stability*. Then he was no longer dominated by any desire, addictive or otherwise.

We have to make efforts, of course, but they won't succeed. Let's put it this way, in the end the best effort is no effort. It is to be totally receptive. But that does not mean we do not try to collaborate with the divine action and with life as it unfolds. We simply do not depend on our own good deeds to get there. We see more and more our mixed motivation and the influence of the false self, even in performing good deeds. Effort is important in the beginning, but at some point there is a significant shift in centering prayer and similar meditation practices. As one places all one's confidence in God, prayer becomes effortless. Contemplative prayer, according to John of the Cross, is completely receptive.

Effortless effectiveness is based on great confidence in God, which is learned through our growing awareness and acceptance of the fact that we cannot do it ourselves. The feeling of powerlessness keeps growing stronger. I am not talking about a low self-image or some psychological pathology, or the period of adolescence, when one needs to develop a strong ego to deal with ordinary life.

As we grow older, we exhaust the various archetypes that belong to human growth during our adolescent period. A great deal of wisdom is present in the archetypes, depending on how they are presented and how we understand them.

The integration of all the capacities of human nature makes for the kind of simplicity we are speaking of here. The more experience we have of God's activity, the more likely we are for divine union. God is not just one thing, but infinite possibilities.

In the animal world, one interesting example that evolution provides is that certain animals developed a marvelous capacity to defend themselves or to get food, like the saber-toothed tiger. It was the less differentiated species however, that continued to evolve into higher species, and eventually into us. Through nature, God seems to be saying,

"I take care of trillions of different species and I will be able to provide for you."

As one aspires to the transforming union and beyond, we must leave to God the decision as to whether we reach enlightenment in this life or not. He does not want us to *desire* enlightenment because as we saw we might fall into the temptation to seek it on our own terms. God insists on his terms for transformation, because they are the only way that works!

The sense of powerlessness is perhaps our greatest treasure, provided we are not overwhelmed by it. In the night of spirit one may at times feel suspended over an abyss of nothingness, with nothing to stand on and unable to protect oneself from the waves of distress, humiliation, or interior doubts that are flowing over us like tidal waves. That is a participation in the mystery of Christ's descent into hell. As the Swiss theologian Hans Urs von Balthasar wrote, it is the precise moment of the redemption of the world.

When we feel utterly overwhelmed by our sinfulness or the experience of the abyss, we are closest to Christ. Having tasted utter weakness, we are prepared to receive everything as sheer gift.

Inside the experience of our nothingness is the reality of transformation. Just beyond what we think or experience as unbearable is the experience of interior freedom and beatitude. Death is not the end of life, but the birth canal into eternal life. The experience of our emptiness is not annihilation, but the death of the false self and resurrection into eternal life and divine union.➤

# EPILOGUE

## ARCHETYPES OF HUMAN DEVELOPMENT

THE SPIRITUAL PILGRIMAGE is not fully engaged by developmental psychology, though it is a great tool. The spiritual dimension of life has to be added for self-knowledge to be complete. The so-called archetypes are another way of understanding human development. Archetypes are an insight of the Swiss psychologist Carl Jung. In his view they are the patrimony of the whole human family because they appear in almost every known culture in the world *with a certain order.* If we skip over one of the archetypes, the Divine Therapist may take us back to complete it. We need to encounter and pass through all the archetypes in some degree to fully grasp and integrate the special qualities of each of them into the spiritual journey.

### The Orphan

The archetype of the Orphan manifests profound security and survival needs. In the beginning, a child depends completely on others, especially parents, to survive from day to day, hour to hour, and moment to moment. This helplessness may be expressed by gestures that plead for help, such as, *Please take care of me*, implying, *I can't take care of myself.* This paralyzing inertia can lead to a passive, dependent personality, which is usually the result of oppression from dominating or over-strict parents, teachers, or cultural influences, or having to compete for affection and attention in an orphanage or substitute family. Prolonged rejection or oppression leads the child to feeling unwanted, unloved, and worthless, locked into a low self-image, and over-fearful of making mistakes. The Orphan is focused on the gratification of its emotional program for security and survival.

### The Warrior

To be a warrior was highly esteemed in patriarchal times by those eager to fight for themselves and others' rights as they saw them. Warriors have strong egos. They love to compete and to make waves in society. They enjoy winning and the pleasure of dominating others and situations; they despise weakness in themselves and other people. They are willing to fight for what they see as worthy causes. They hate defeat or failure, especially in their own eyes. They depend on the energy of anger to enable them to persevere in pursuing the difficult good, to overcome every sign of cowardice in themselves, and to defend special causes they may have embraced. The Warrior is focused on its emotional program for power and control.

Is the desire or willingness to kill innate in human nature? The power of life and death over another person is the ultimate symbol of dominion over others. Scapegoating relieves the guilt feelings that arise from killing or wanting to kill, but it does not take away those negative feelings.

Proving oneself in battle was historically the chief badge of honor for men at one time. The warrior energy especially in recent times is primarily channeled into the will to succeed (high achieving) and the imitation of models on the athletic field, academic success in school, and prominence in the workplace. Integrity for the warrior may express itself by keeping his word, whatever the cost to himself and to others.

At present, with nuclear weapons threatening the survival of civilization as we know it, war can no longer be used as in the past as a rite of passage to manhood. Archetypes are pervasive forms, but their particular expression is shaped by the general level of consciousness of a particular historical time and culture.

### The Martyr

The Martyr as victim or altruist is an archetype that Western culture has in the past considered to be women's traditional domain. Frequent characteristics: to serve others or some cause even when it is beyond one's strength; to try to please everyone and never to displease anyone; to sacrifice oneself even to the point of death; to feel obliged inwardly to carry the world on one's shoulders. Other symptoms might be: never to complain; to practice unquestioning and blind obedience to religious superiors; to put up with endless unfair criticism; and to be excessively loyal to a cause or group identity that one wholeheartedly espouses, like patriotism, religion, or family.

People usually possess a strong tendency to conform to the accepted norms of their society or to the group with which they most identify. The Martyr is reluctant to accept help and can rarely refuse requests or say no.

In our time, psychology has identified the Martyr archetype with pathology. It is now socially unacceptable in the West as an ideal.

### The Wanderer

The Wanderer is exemplified by the life of the historical Buddha, who was raised in a rich and noble household, taken care of from morning till night, and allowed to enjoy every pleasure without accountability. He was being prepared to rule the castle or the fiefdom after his parents retired or passed on.

Then, all on the same day according to the tradition, the Buddha happened to encounter a corpse, an aged person, and a very sick person—sights he had never witnessed before in his life and that horrified him. He decided to give up pleasure-seeking and joined a group of ascetics in the forest near his home. There he lived a life of intense ascetical discipline for several years.

Neither lifestyle brought him happiness. Disillusioned by both a life of luxury and one of severe asceticism, he emerged from the forest, sat down under a bodhi tree, and embraced *just being*. He then received one of the great religious enlightenments of all time. He spent the rest of his life teaching what he called the Middle Way, along with the Four Noble Truths and the Eightfold Path of Buddhist practice.

The Wanderer is one who has not found happiness as an Orphan, Warrior, or Martyr. He or she sets out to experiment, to see the world, and to leave the safety of home and family, the athletic field, one's peer group, and the conventional morality of the local culture. Some begin this wandering journey in adolescence. Others pursue it for most of their lives or as long as they can. Those who cannot travel may express this archetype by joining self-help groups or trying different meditation techniques, religions, or no religion. Their wandering stems from their overarching desire to find their True Self, or to experience complete independence as an ideal. Some may be genuinely seeking the truth. This archetype will attract and absorb an adventurous personality and may involve sexual promiscuity for a time as one of its expressions.

## *The Magician*

The Magician has tried and experienced these early archetypes and is ready to move beyond them into the rational level of consciousness, which is to graduate from all the preceding archetypes that one has experienced and found wanting. This is to move beyond adolescence and into adulthood. The lower instincts are now in some degree integrated into the specifically human faculties of intellect and will. The faculties of sense are designed to defer decision-making to the rational powers. One does not reject the positive values of the previous archetypes, but is now open to the further development of the spiritual capacities of the human organism and the evolving brain.

One is now ready to commit oneself to long-range goals, to take full responsibility for oneself and one's behavior, and to commit to the service of others. Ideally, this takes place for human beings around their twenty-first birthday, but in Western cultures it is delayed, as present-day adolescence becomes more prolonged. To make permanent commitments before this stage is well established could lead to failure and to doing more harm than good, both to oneself and to the lives of others.

The natural and infused moral virtues may appear as this archetype evolves:

a) Prudence is taking adequate steps leading up to decision-taking.

b) Fortitude (courage) is persevering in the difficult good in order to attain one's goals.

c) Justice is rendering to everyone what is each one's due.

d) Temperance consists in moderating one's instinctual and emotional desires and energies.

Occasional signs of the Fruits and Gifts of the Spirit may also occur. They enable one to recognize and accept what is true about oneself and others. To be honest and open to the present moment makes one profoundly vulnerable. Personal integrity requires passing beyond over-identification with one or all of the archetypes.

### The Saint

The Saint is an alchemist in the medieval sense, one who transforms the world by transforming oneself. The Saint is also called the Magician by some authors. This is one who continuously and faithfully fulfills the duties of his or her state of life.

The Saint is capable of teaching the way of transformation, but cannot yet transmit it to others. He or she teaches by their example. The divine action is very powerful in them. They are advanced students in the science of love, and they keep progressing in love's refinements and creativity.

All the other archetypes, except that of the Sage and

King or Queen, are now integrated. The saints live life in a divine-human way motivated more and more by divine love, which seeks no reward. For them, loving God is its own reward. They are forgetful of the emotional programs for happiness of the false self and are habitually aware of being in union with God. They also feel oneness with all creation, especially other people. This is the fully Christian life and the death of the separate-self sense. The latter might be described as "no fixed point of reference."

The Saints are moved by the Fruits and Gifts of the Spirit rather than by their egos. They are not overly attached to anything. They are non-possessive of themselves, their talents, and even of their experiences of God. Christ lives and acts in them and pours the Spirit into them uninterruptedly. In the deepest sense, Christ *is* them and they are Christ. This archetype marks the return to innocence of which the biblical Garden of Eden is the symbol. Those who have reached this stage experience the goodness of the universe and of people as they grow in contemplation and mature as human beings.

The Saint is ready to contribute to the transformation of society. There is no nest or niche to hide in anymore, while expecting the leader of the group to decide everything. Personal integrity requires taking responsibility for oneself and living under the influence and guidance of one's true self.

The Saint's task is to bring peace and new life to their ailing cultures. The symptoms of the true self are well developed at this archetypal stage, especially through the exercise of the Fruits and Gifts of the Spirit. The latter in the Christian tradition are manifested by the Beatitudes. The Gift of Counsel, for example, enhances the infused virtue of prudence and directs all one's actions even in great detail. One begins to accept and to love one's weakness, while at the same time placing all one's trust in God's healing and transforming grace. Synchronicity becomes a frequent expectation as one works out the details of living, decision-making, and decision-taking under the guidance of the Spirit. Timing is perceived to be an important factor for any kind of service or ministry. The Saint has learned how to wait for God (see Isaiah 30:15).

### The Sage

The Sage is a person emerging as a further development of the archetype of Saint. Highly evolved people have the Gift of Wisdom, which shares its inspirations with both the intellect and will and unifies all the powers of the human continuum of body, soul, and spirit. Sages also feel unified with everyone else. They feel at one with God, the whole human family, and with all creation. They are like the monks described in the desert spirituality of the fourth century as "separated from all and united to all." In other words, they have become one with all that is. By becoming nothing—detached from every possession including spiritual gifts—they have become everything. They can now transmit the divine life by their simple presence as well as by their teaching.

Sages can leave behind the merely cultural aspects of their religion without rejecting them. They are no longer unduly dependent on ritual and prefer silence to words in relating to God. They have become one with the Oneness to which all religious practices point: life in the present moment and communion in the continuous and conscious presence of God in them and in all reality.

### The King or Queen

The *King* or *Queen* usually experiences a period of prolonged solitude and intense silence, after which they return to the marketplace and enrich many. They are not only teachers but freely transmit the experience of what they teach. They are peacemakers, mediators between God and the community, and priests in the fullest sense of the term, who inspire and empower those they encounter to serve God and each other. They do not rule by force, but their very presence is authoritative. Possessing the divine presence without any possessive attitude, they communicate God appropriately in every situation. They are not dominating or authoritarian. By manifesting God as the servant of creation, they become examples of what servant leadership actually is.

The King or Queen leads without leading; they have lost their individual selves as fixed points of reference. They have experienced all the archetypes and their integration. For the King and Queen there is no danger of getting stuck in earlier archetypes.

The King or Queen empowers others, easily delegates authority, and seems to do nothing while accomplishing much. They manifest the innate authority of integrated personal experience. They have no attachment to their role and exercise servant leadership by means of their total gift of themselves to God and to the people they serve, and with consummate skill manifest the commandment to love one's neighbor.

The King and Queen are wisdom teachers chiefly by their silence. They exemplify the statement of Paul, "as poor, yet making many rich; as having nothing, and yet possessing everything" (2 Corinthians 6:10). In their own eyes, they are weak and powerless. They manifest in daily life the divine way of being human. They are unobtrusive, but universally loved; fully individuated and at the same time person-oriented. They are translators of God's will into the nitty-gritty of daily life with its myriad details. They live ordinary lives with extraordinary love.

Like God, they are always active and always at rest. They possess and enjoy peace in the midst of turmoil and inner freedom in every situation. They practice boundless compassion, limitless forgiveness, always showing mercy, and continuously channeling divine love visibly and invisibly into the human family past, present, and to come. They are the servants of all and the epitome of emptiness; yet they find enjoyment in everything. Limitless longing for the pure love of God is what most characterizes the spirituality of the archetype of King or Queen. The King or Queen is rooted in their spiritual tradition, but always poised for constructive and, if needed, revolutionary change. ◆

# ABOUT
# CONTEMPLATIVE OUTREACH

CONTEMPLATIVE OUTREACH is a spiritual network of individuals and small-faith communities committed to living the contemplative dimension of the Gospel. The common desire for Divine transformation, primarily expressed through a commitment to a daily centering prayer practice, unites its international and interdenominational community.

Today Contemplative Outreach annually serves over 40,000 people; supports over 120 active contemplative chapters in 39 countries; supports over 800 prayer groups; teaches over 15,000 people the practice of centering prayer and other contemplative practices through locally hosted workshops; and provides training and resources to local chapters and volunteers. Contemplative Outreach also publishes and distributes the teachings of Fr. Thomas Keating and other resources that support centering prayer and the contemplative life.

For more information about Contemplative Outreach, visit www.contemplativeoutreach.org.

# ABOUT
# LANTERN BOOKS

LANTERN BOOKS was founded in 1999 on the principle of living with a greater depth and commitment to the preservation of the natural world. In addition to publishing books on animal advocacy, vegetarianism, religion, and environmentalism, Lantern is dedicated to printing books in the U.S. on recycled paper and saving resources in day-to-day operations. Lantern is honored to be a recipient of the highest standard in environmentally responsible publishing from the Green Press Initiative.

LANTERNBOOKS.COM